What if..?

How to Create the Life You Want Using the *Power of Possibility*

MARTINA E. FAULKNER, LMSW

nspireBytes Press

What If..?

How to Create the Life You Want
Using the Power of Possibility
by Martina E. Faulkner, LMSW

978-0-9963668-0-9
978-0-9963668-1-6 (hardcover)
978-0-9963668-2-3 (ebook)

Library of Congress Control Number: 2015906936

Cover and interior design by Michelle Radomski, OneVoiceCan.com

Author's photo by Charlotte DiNunzio

nspireBytes Press

www.inspirebytes.com
www.martinafaulkner.com

For my mom,
who has supported and
encouraged me in my dreams.

Here's the thing about dreams:
They are fueled by the power of
infinite possibility.

To Mary Anne,
Happy daydreaming!
xoxo
Martha

Acknowledgments

To my clients who continue to amaze me every day
with their commitment to themselves

To my teachers and mentors who held me up
along the way, sharing their wisdom,
experience, and presence

To my beta reading group—Ali, Andy, Julie, Kim,
Lois, and Teri—for your encouragement,
feedback, and time

To Kate, for your editorial expertise,
providing valuable insight,
and sharing in this process with me

To Michelle, my publisher, for recognizing
my vision and walking me through
the final stages of creation

To Sally, for your extraordinary creative
management skills and talents
in helping me bring my work to the world

To José for being a valued colleague and mentor,
for your encouragement, support, and belief in me

To my friends and family for supporting me
and having the patience to share
in this journey with me

And finally, to my parents, whose love and
support helped make this journey possible

Thank you.

Table of Contents

Foreword

What if you were to read a powerful and yet sweet book that could transform your entire approach to life? Many great people of the past understood the principles that Martina Faulkner speaks of in this concise gem of a book about manifesting through the question **"What if..?"**. Great inventors like Thomas Edison, Washington Carver, the Wright brothers, Leonardo Da Vinci, Tesla, Charles Babbage, Archimedes, Alexander Bell, Steve Jobs, and a host of others knew the power of asking open questions and made liberal use of the method. And thereby did many powerful explorers, emperors, teachers, religious leaders, and generals realize great dreams that changed history. They each had powerful curiosity and wanted to know what was possible and how to do something never accomplished before. And they were amazingly successful, so successful, in fact, that their discoveries and exploits changed the entire world in a single generation. It was not that these individuals were somehow smarter and or more realized than everyone else. They were using the same basic skills that everyone uses to live their lives. They had the ability to think, feel, and act just like you do. The difference was that they had an unwavering focus, were extremely curious, were powerfully passionate to know, and were all highly persistent.

However, not all of these now-famous individuals were able to find happiness through their accomplishments. Some were driven by ego, some by religious fervor, some by the desire to serve. To the degree that they were driven by altruistic motives, they were more likely to find fulfillment, satisfaction, and happiness, and to the degree that they were driven by ego to realize personal gain over others, they often met with catastrophic or disappointing ends—think of Alexander the Great, Hitler, Napoleon, and Rasputin, to name just a few.

These historical figures knew enough to manifest what they wanted, or thought they wanted, for better or worse. They may have intuitively known the right method, happened upon it by chance, or learned the principles from their great teachers. This information has always been available to those dedicated to finding out. You need not stumble through trial and error to painstakingly discover what works.

Martina has done the preliminary research for you, gathered it up, and made it available in an organized, clear, and focused, step-by-step process, to help you manifest your dreams effectively and quickly. The best part is that she cuts out all the gobbledygook that accompanies most other books on the subject of manifesting and focuses on the essentials. She skips the long explanations and gets down to the nitty-gritty through exercises and questioning — processes that work exceptionally well. And best of all, she personalizes the process with examples from her own experience, both positive and negative.

Martina has clearly done her own required emotional homework and this qualifies her to write this book from an authoritative, mature, and compassionate perspective. As an added bonus, she is a trained and qualified counselor, healer, and teacher.

And oh yes, there is one more thing. Martina is not afraid to say it like it is. She is not afraid to tell the truth, even if it means you might be disappointed or it might contradict something you hope is true or not true. This is always the sign of someone you can trust, someone who is clear and loving enough to skip the ingratiation and whitewash and instead, educate you. Enjoy.

José Luis Stevens, PhD, co-founder of the Power Path School of Shamanism and author of *Awaken the Inner Shaman*, *The Power Path*, *Secrets of Shamanism*, and *Transforming your Dragons*.

Why "What if..?"

This chapter could also be titled: "Why does what you say matter?" The easy answer is: choice.

Once I completed the preliminary manuscript, I beta-tested the book on a small group of readers with a cross-section of professions, age, and gender. One result of that exercise was this chapter on why this book is so important, and how this concept created change in my own life.

To begin with, this is a book about empowerment, choice, and change. It's an introduction to using manifesting as a tool to become the conductor of your own life as well as the importance of recognizing the sheer power of possibility.

Even without employing the more metaphysical idea of "manifesting," this is a book about choice and change.

How do you choose to live?

How are you choosing to show up in your own life? In others' lives?

What do you choose to do on a daily basis to support your dreams and goals?

How conscious are you of the choices you make?

Life is about choice.

Now let's go back to the conductor metaphor. Let's say you have an orchestra at your disposal. Perhaps it's a string quartet, or maybe it's the New York Philharmonic. Either way, it's yours. We all have one. Some orchestras are well-tuned while others are just getting started.

What would happen if we threw a bunch of musicians together, with no sheet music, and asked them to play together? My guess is there might be some dissonance. There might even be a few musicians who walk out. There might also be some beautiful music, but we're leaving a lot up to chance in that scenario.

Now, what if we were able to hand everybody the same sheet music and invite them to play together? What kind of music would we create then? We have the option of using existing compositions or creating our own. The sky is the limit actually, and the choice is ours.

As the conductor of our own life, it falls upon us to create the music we want to hear and live with on a daily basis. It becomes a question of choice.

The quality of our life is based on the choices we make.

We all have choice. We get to choose how we want to show up for ourselves and others every day. Beyond that, we get to partner with the Universe to expand on the possibilities for our lives. That is what this book is about: empowerment and change through choice.

Now, why should you read it? Or, why should you trust me when I tell you this is powerful? Because I've experienced it firsthand, both personally and professionally.

For years I have worked to explore, understand, and experience various modalities of spirituality and wellness. I started my own journey more than a decade ago, and I slowly built up my own personal and professional toolboxes. The tools I use represent a cross-section of the wellness industry, and I work to synthesize them all into manageable and accessible nuggets of information for my clients and readers. In fact, my first coaching business was called Synthesis Life Coaching for that very reason.

Learning something new is always exciting and full of hope. It can also be challenging. My goal in sharing what I've learned and used is to help make that process easier and more accessible. This book is one such example.

I invite you to try it out for yourself. In the pages that follow **you'll learn how to explore your own inner workings, beliefs, and values and how you can create meaningful change in your life in a way that is in alignment with your core values and your soul's purpose.** This book can serve as a guide. I've detailed myriad ways in which you can use this book for your benefit. The only limit is the one you create.

I am happy and grateful this book is in your hands and that we get to spend this time together. Now, let's get to work creating something magical!

What and If?

What if..?

"What if..?" is a simple little phrase that belies its greatness. It is an incredibly powerful tool that can be used to manifest the greatest joys or undermine even the most assured confidence. It all depends on how you use it.

Two benign words in their own right. Six small letters. Harmless apart, but when combined, "what" and "if" can be equally creative and destructive.

Let me explain:

"What if..?" makes the entirety of the Universe possible by accessing the most creative and infinite power of all: imagination. As a tool for exploration and innovation, these two little words open up endless possibilities. Dreams become realities.

However, **"What if..?"**, when used in fear or hindsight, becomes a potential harbinger of shame, blame, and despair: The "shoulda-coulda-woulda" of that which was not done or seen. It exposes its user to the insecurities harbored in the mind.

In the Universe, there is a unity and duality to everything. They are not mutually exclusive. You, yourself, are whole, and you are also comprised of both the light and the dark—yin and yang. In other words: unity and duality. Similarly, there is a duality to the phrase **"What if..?"**.

It may help to think of it this way: a star is simultaneously expanding and contracting. For us, the sun is a life force giving us light and warmth, helping things grow and live. And yet, it is also contracting and will eventually implode and die. As with all things, it is both living and dying. It is expanding and contracting. It contains a duality in its unity.

This phrase is the same. It is both creative and destructive. It is a singular phrase with an inherent duality.

Six letters, two words, powerful beyond measure... and *what separates how they are used is you.*

How it All Began

This book started as a nagging idea while I was finishing up my graduate degree in social work. As I worked with clients, I knew that I wanted to blend my certifications in Coaching and Reiki with my degree as a psychotherapist. On the one hand, I wanted to help them explore everything that's possible—their dreams, their desires, and their hopes. On the other hand, I also wanted to assist them in unpacking and exploring their past and the reasons why they found themselves where they were when they came to me.

"What if..?" was a question that could be used in both instances, and I heard myself doing just that.

"What if you hadn't..?"
"What if you could..?"
"What if you weren't/didn't or were/did..?"

As I continued using it more deliberately in client sessions, I started to really understand the power behind these two little words.

Fast-forward many months and **"What if..?"** started to play a bigger role in my own life—as if this book was trying to write itself (which it sort of did). Time and time again the phrase popped into my head or was somewhere in my environment. It took one last nudge for me to sit down and start typing.

I'll always be grateful to José Stevens for that last little push to put words to paper. José is a gifted advisor and teacher, having created The Power Path School of Shamanism from years of study and experience. During our last phone conversation, José said to me:

"I want you to try something. I want you to say **'What if..'** *and then add whatever it is you can think of, beyond what you even desire."*

You know when you hear something over and over again, and although you're hearing it you're not actually hearing it? Then one day someone or something comes along and says it again and it's like—Boom!—there it is in the forefront of your being?

This was it! Someone had asked me to use the tool myself. Not only was it a meaningful exercise for me, but it was the last little push I needed to finally write this book and share this powerful tool with others.

I like to think that this book was marinating somewhere until it was ready (or I was ready) to get cooking. The result is something delicious: a thought-provoking exercise in imagination and manifestation. A journey into possibility. I hope it proves equally as exciting for you as it was for me once I started employing the actual power of the phrase.

And it all begins with two little words:

What if..?

CHAPTER 1

How to Use This Book

"Start where you are. Use what you have. Do what you can."

— Arthur Ashe —

We read most things cover to cover. It's how we were taught to experience a book. Indeed, most books are written in a progressive narrative, building on the pages that came before. This is not such a book. Not entirely.

This is a book that is meant to be used.

What do I mean by that?

Once you've read the opening chapters (1–5) explaining the concept, the rest of the book is at your disposal to read as you are inspired. That means you can pick it up at any point after chapter 5 based on your current situation and needs. Or you can allow the Universe to guide you to what would be most beneficial. I've done that with many a book and have always gotten what I need when I have trusted enough to let go and allow myself to be guided.

How did I do that?

Well, what if you sat down, put the book spine down on your lap, closed your eyes, and let it fall open to a random page? What if you allowed yourself to trust in that process, and you opened your eyes to read whatever words you saw without actively searching for them? Then, what if it was exactly what you needed to hear?

Whether you're holding this book in your lap, or scrolling through on an e-reader, what if you sat quietly, moved your finger through the pages, and stopped when it felt right? That's how I advise you to use this book. Use it, don't "read" it.

Of course, you can read it straight through if you want, or chapter by chapter based on what you need.

Both ways are equally effective and important. In fact, you can do it one way, and then go back and do it the other. As with all things in life, the power of choice is yours. Just as it is with how you formulate your phrases around the concept of **What if..?.**

You get to choose.

The one caveat, as I've already mentioned, is that it is a good idea to read the opening chapters to get a greater understanding of the concept before jumping into using the book in the way that best suits your needs.

After completing the opening chapters (1–5), you'll find each subsequent chapter contains the same approach to a different topic. They each start with a series of questions to get you thinking and connected to the topic at hand. From there I employ exercises and share ideas and information to help you expand your process. Finally, they each end with a summary to help solidify the ideas you've just explored. Some chapters are longer than others. Some may be of interest to you while others may not. That's ok. The overview and material presented initially may not seem very deep, but the work you are invited to do can be profound. Again, it's all in how you choose to use it.

So let's get started.

CHAPTER 2

The Power of Possibility

"It is better to believe than to disbelieve; in doing you bring everything to the realm of possibility."

— *Albert Einstein* —

What is The Power of Possibility, and what does all this mean?

We're going to get a little science-y now. Everything —everything—carries potential within it. Everything is comprised of energy. We're all little balls of energy wandering around a rock made up of energy, floating in a Universe comprised of energy.

Well, that's a REALLY simple way to look at it, but it works. As I started to go further into the details of energy and matter, I realized the importance of simplifying things in order to understand the concept of the Power of Possibility and its role in manifesting. Here are some basics that I have distilled from my readings:

Everything has energy. Energy can't be created or destroyed; it can only be transferred. There are different types of energy, specifically potential energy and kinetic energy. Typically, everything has potential energy until that something is put into use or activated, and then it becomes kinetic energy. Once it's dormant again, it reverts to potential energy. Nothing is lost or gained; it is merely transformed temporarily.

So, in many ways, energy is in everything and everything uses energy. But energy itself is not a tangible "thing." Therefore, energy is pure potential. It's the essence of possibility and creation. And, since *we* are energy, we also carry the essence of possibility and creation within us. Cool, huh?

That gives us a good place to start. But what does it really mean?

It means that with few exceptions, mostly biological, if you can think of it you can probably do it. Which also means that if you can focus your attention (energy) on something, you are activating it and giving it infinitely more power to come to fruition.

The action of thought transforms the potential into the kinetic, even briefly, which increases the possibility of it manifesting. This applies to everything.

Enter Murphy's Law.

Have you ever noticed how we say things like "Just my luck" and "Wouldn't you know" after something happens that we were hoping wouldn't? We've even given it its own category in life: Murphy's Law.

Actually, Murphy's Law is the idea that anything that can go wrong, eventually will. Colloquially, the connotation has come to describe any and all such adverse outcomes that should have been thought of, or could have been thought of, and are then attributed to mere coincidence. But if we accept the truth that everything has a base energy, it stands to reason that we have the power to call forth even the things we don't actively want simply by thinking of them.

So, here's the big piece we're missing when we attribute unwanted events to coincidence:

If we are putting ANY energy into them at all, we are helping them manifest.

What does this mean, though, with regard to manifesting the life you want in alignment with who you are and what your soul needs?

It means that if you can imagine it—it can happen.

You may not control the "when" of it all, but by putting your energy and focus on it in a healthy and deliberate manner, while keeping the guidelines and Universal laws in mind, you've increased your chances of bringing it forth. Dramatically.

This also means if you spent your time praying and hoping for something *not* to happen, chances are you've just helped it happen. Focusing your energy on anything helps it come about. Murphy's Law.

∞

Now, to put this into practice, let's play a little. Here's a variation of an exercise I was given a long time ago in order to begin to see how The Power of Possibility truly works.

I want you to choose something to focus on. You can get as specific as you like, but it's best to start with something simple. Here's what I did:

I asked the Universe to show me yellow cars. Yellow cars are not a common color on the road, so it seemed that this would be a good test of sorts. For a few days, I focused on seeing yellow cars and inviting them into my sphere. Within a week, the amount of yellow cars I saw as I was driving increased noticeably. It was a bit spooky, actually. I had no idea so many yellow cars existed.

I then took it further. I asked to see two very specific models of cars that are not common: the Toyota FJ Cruiser and the VW Beetle. This was just around the time of the reintroduction of the Beetle, so it wasn't as common as it is today. These were each distinct cars, so it would be easy to notice a change. Lo and behold! Within a week I was seeing more of both. More importantly, however, I also started seeing a lot of *yellow* Beetles and Cruisers. The Universe had kept my previous "order" going as I added on to it. How cool is that?

There are two ways to look at these results:

1. Attribute the results to my increased focus on the specific item, assuming it was there all the while; and/or

2. Attribute the results to the Universe meeting my request and my needs by providing me with what I had requested and manifested into my reality.

I think it's both, actually. The beautiful thing, however, is that it doesn't really matter which one it is. Why? Because in manifesting, we're looking for results, and I got them! If we go about it deliberately and consciously, with good intention, it's a win all around.

∞

So it is with the Power of Possibility. If you can imagine it, you can create it. Now, that doesn't take into account biological boundaries. But barring those few limitations, the Universe is yours to imagine, create, and enjoy. The only confines you have are the borders of your own imagination.

The Power of Possibility is both the engine that fuels the machine that is your imagination, as well as the fuel that feeds the engine. It's everything all at once, and it's cyclical. It's the essence of energy itself. Filled with potential, infinite in its essence, the Power of Possibility is the source of all that is and will be.

Most importantly, the Power of Possibility is housed in your very soul. Everyone has access to it. You're born with it. Watch a child and you'll see how accessible it is. Allow a child to explore with their mind and all borders fall away. Life becomes infinitely possible. Conversely, tell a child "no" and watch them deflate.

Imagination is the human expression of Possibility.

Possibility is the Divine expressed in reality as energy.

The Power of Possibility is the root source of change.

CHAPTER 3

A Little Background

*"For me context is the key—from that comes
the understanding of everything."*

— Kenneth Noland —

In coaching, and in some therapeutic practices, there is
a "magic wand" question. It goes something like this:

*If I gave you a magic wand right now, what would
you choose to change or do?*

It's a tool that helps circumvent old belief systems
and thought patterns when someone is stuck. Using
a magic wand question cuts to the chase by asking a

big question at a time when someone feels mired in minutiae.

What if..? is a magic wand on steroids.

When used to unlock the creative flow, it can open you up to the Power of Possibility and manifesting or creating a life you may have never even dreamed of. In fact, it goes beyond dreams and taps into the essence of who we are at a soul level.

In a series of ten essays, I have explored the potential behind the phrase using specific scenarios. These are some of the most common issues facing clients I work with, clients my colleagues work with (I asked), and that I see reflected in the media, including social media. I invite you to create your own, in your own words, based on your situation, using these as a guide.

Now here's the cautionary tale, as I've already mentioned: **What if..?** can also be incredibly destructive. It can undermine even the strongest prayer, and it can rip apart dreams and build a hole so deep it seems almost impossible to climb out. Therefore, it's important to have a good grasp and understanding of the process before you jump in. As with everything, a little knowledge can go a long way.

Here are some examples of the destructive side of **What if..?**:

What if...

- I don't get into college?
- He/she doesn't love me?
- I get sick?
- I fail?
- I lose everything?
- I'm forever alone?

You get the point. I don't want to add all that negative energy into the Universe, so I'll simply say 'cancel and purify' right now to mitigate what I just wrote. *(P.S. That's a handy little phrase for undoing a negative thought you might have had. I've used it for years, and it is now second nature—as much a part of my lexicon as hello.)*

You see what I'm saying, though, don't you? **What if..?** can lead you down two paths; each paved with their own energy and emotion. My advice is to choose the path that makes you smile as you're speaking or thinking the words. If it makes your heart happy, it's probably a good choice.

Only you can choose how to use this phrase, but there are a few guidelines to manifesting that can make it even more effective and enjoyable in the process.

∞

The Guidelines

To begin with, here's a summary of the manifesting guidelines in list format so that you can refer to it as often as you need to. *(For those of you using an e-reader, you might want to bookmark this page.)*

1. Start small.
2. Write it down.
3. Use action words.
4. Use the positive expression of a word.
5. Take ownership.
6. Be consistent and repetitive.
7. Use visualization.
8. Feelings matter.
9. "Or better."
10. Be open.

Now let's go a little deeper into each guideline.

1. Start small. Going from 0 to 100 isn't healthy. It's also not practical. Why? Because it very rarely lasts. Think of it this way: If someone were to remove you entirely from your situation and put you on a deserted island with a private chef, a trainer, and a meditation guru, you'd feel refreshed and renewed very quickly. You'd be reconnecting with yourself, living optimally, and experiencing true joy and wellness. This is the likelihood of what that experience will bring you. (I know, I did this with a personal retreat.) And then you'd have to return to your current situation, and in a matter of days or weeks everything you learned and did would slowly be replaced and/or pushed aside by your original reality. Only now you'd have a bit of a hangover from the joy you experienced, and you might even feel less joy than you did before you left. It's possible, if not probable. Trust me.

Early on in my quest for understanding I tried this technique. Hindsight has given me the wisdom to know it doesn't work. Deliberate integration of learning, in small steps, over a period of time, is the best way to create change.

Actually, this is very much a social work idea: meet people where they are, within their environment. Help them within their existing reality. Why? Because it gives them the tools for success within their environment, which may ultimately help them to change their situation. This is a foundation of true change. So, do yourself a favor and start small.

Don't, however, read that as "stay small" or "don't dream big" because that's not what I'm saying. Make your dreams *huge*; let them be whatever they want to be. With the manifestation practice, when you're beginning it makes sense to start small. It's the difference between saying: "What if I had the body of a fitness expert?" and "What if I were healthier?" See the difference? Small steps lead to great and lasting change. We may not all be supermodels, but we can all feel like supermodels, which is more likely when we feel healthy.

2. Write it down. Actually, keep a journal. Keep a journal that's just for you and your **What if..?** practice. I ask all my clients to keep a journal of our work and time together. Why? For two reasons:

A. It helps to have a place to record your ideas and thoughts as they are happening. Keeping the journal with you at all times as a place to jot down whatever is popping into your mind as you begin this process is an invaluable tool. A journal frees up the real estate in your mind to create more, think more, imagine more.

B. A journal shows you progress over time. Too often I've seen clients who have made great changes in their lives, only to entirely forget that they have these accomplishments under their belt. A journal eliminates this problem and reinforces the positive progress we make along the way, which serves to reinforce our journey and the power of our decisions and intuition.

3. **Use action words.** Action words say something. They are statements of willingness and investment.

They define whatever follows them with ownership and emphasis. Take a look at these two phrases and see how different they feel when you read each of them:

"What if I were healthier?" vs. "What if I ate healthier?"

Grammar aside, the feeling behind the second phrase implies accountability, involves ownership, and takes action. It is much more powerful, and it's also easier to access the visualizations associated with eating than it is with being (see Guideline 7). Now, let's use the same example and see why it's not in your best interest to include "wanting" in your manifestation. Here are two phrases again:

"**What if** I wanted to be healthier?" vs. "**What if** I were healthier?" (Yes, I used the "were" phrase in that one to show how "want" is even less powerful than "were.")

Using "want" in your manifestation is the equivalent of asking to be in a perpetual state of "wanting" or desire, never quite achieving whatever it is you're asking for. This demonstrates the importance of picking strong verbs and words. Action words are stronger than passive words, and passive words are stronger than "wanting." It's a spectrum. Where you choose to be on the spectrum directly impacts the scope of your possible results.

So, can you feel the difference when you use action words? It's powerful, isn't it? Not only does it directly impact how we feel, it also nudges us into more investment. More investment and more action are powerful nuances that require very little of us in advance and can pay off greatly later.

Finally, be picky! Choose wisely, and explore your options using those amazing tools you have right there in your body: your imagination and your brain.

4. Use the positive expression of a word. (aka: Don't use double negatives.) This is very much a NLP thing. (NLP = Neuro-Linguistic Programming) The energy in each word matters. Additionally, the energy in a phrase matters. In other words, you can't use two negatives to make a positive. Here's an example:

"**What if** I don't get sick?" vs. "**What if** I am healthy?"

In the "don't get sick" phrase, you have two negatives—"don't" and "sick"—working to create a positive, but they never quite get there. Furthermore, the Universe doesn't always understand the double negative, especially when focusing on providing results. What the Universe may hear is "get sick" and then respond with, "Ok, if that's what you really want." We don't, of course, which means it's up to us to be clear with our words and phrasing.

Keeping the positive expression of a word, instead of using a negative qualifier, is more active, direct, and focused. Therefore, it is also more powerful.

5. Take ownership. This is the difference between "I" and "it." As an example, it's more powerful to say "**What if** I ate more healthfully?" than "**What if** my life were healthier?"

It's important to emphasize the role ownership plays in manifesting and opening yourself up to the Power of Possibility. Ownership is the equivalent of raising your hand and standing up when someone asks for a volunteer.

We've all been in those meetings or gatherings when the speaker asks for a volunteer and nobody steps up. If you're like most people (myself included at one point in my life), you sink a little into your seat when that happens. Ownership is the opposite of sinking. It's about showing up and jumping up. Of course, it's important to do so wisely, which is why your words matter.

Owning your manifestation is an exclamation point to the Universe. It demonstrates your willingness to participate in the process and receive. It shows openness and integrity. Who wouldn't want to support that?

6. Be consistent and repetitive. It doesn't matter when you choose to do your manifesting; it matters that you do it consistently. I currently do it in the shower or bath. The water helps me find stillness inside and allows me to daydream. Daydreaming is a powerful form of manifesting because it unleashes the imagination. A tethered imagination is nothing to write home about. On the other hand, a free imagination is something quite extraordinary.

So, I daydream a little to see where my ideas can take me. Sometimes this leads to a modification of my manifestation statement, but usually it just underscores it with a whole lot of fun visualizations. Once I've done that, my mind is ready to state, see, and feel the manifestation. So, I settle into the phrase I have created, and I speak it. Sometimes out loud, sometimes silently to myself. (I've even taken to writing it in the condensation on the shower wall!)

Many of my teachers along the way have shared with me that speaking it aloud is more powerful. I'm not going to split hairs about this. If what works for you is speaking it softly or silently, that's what works. If it's better for you to state it loudly and clearly, then by all means, go for it!

Again, what matters is that you do it enough to get into the habit of it. If that's first thing in the morning over a cup of coffee, that's great. If that's on your lunch break as you sit quietly at your desk, also good. What works for you is what works. Enough said.

7. Use visualization. So, this is where the whole "seeing is believing or believing is seeing" comes into question. In truth, when it comes to manifesting, that's a chicken/egg dilemma. What matters most is that you visualize the desired outcome of your manifestation. This means that you need to have an image in your mind's eye that you hold onto as you are stating your manifestation. Hold that vision and speak the words. Seeing it while saying it gives it life. It's like blowing on an ember to create a flame. It helps. A lot.

If this is something that's really challenging for you, I invite you to create a vision board. Here's the catch with vision boards, though: too often, we create a vision board from our ego. This isn't helpful. Years ago, I developed a process that circumvents the ego mind and gets to the heart of the matter with the subconscious. In my opinion, that's the best way to approach a vision board. *(To learn more about this process you can visit my website at www.martinafaulkner.com.)*

In the meantime, to get ideas for your visualization, leaf through the pages of a magazine while thinking or speaking your manifestation. If something jumps out at you, kind of hits you in the gut, grab that image and use it for visualizing. It's a good place to start if you're having some trouble. If they've been underactive for a while, our imaginations sometimes need a little jumpstart to get going again. Once you have one or two images to work with, you'll start generating your own.

8. Feelings matter. Now that you have a phrase and an image, the next step is one that others have alluded to many times over: it's time to experience how it feels in your body at the outcome of your manifestation, both emotionally and physically. What that means is that you need to ask yourself how it feels to be healthier, to use the earlier example. Then actually feel it—in your joints, your muscles, your skin, your body, your breath, and your heart. If you need to start with words, that's okay. We've all learned over time to repress our feelings, so they, too, might need a little jumpstart.

Repeatedly answer the question "How does it feel to...?" to drill down to the emotions and sensations the manifestation brings. To continue with the example of "feeling healthier," that might look like this:

How does it feel to be healthier?

It feels good to be healthier.
It feels liberating to be healthier.
It feels powerful to be healthier.
I feel balanced.

I feel hopeful.

I feel empowered.

I feel grateful.

I feel joy.

I feel strong.

I feel sexy.

I feel happy.

I feel alive.

And on and on. You get the point. (I also hope you noticed the change from "It" to "I.")

9. "Or better." This is an important phrase to add to any manifestation, whether you use the **"What if..?"** process or another one.

"Or better" is the phrase that we state at the end of our intention that opens everything up to the true Power of Possibility. It removes any and all limits from the Universe to meet your needs, and it empowers it to surprise you with something that you couldn't have, or wouldn't have, thought of by yourself.

This is a key element to manifesting that helps to mitigate any human error. Just in case you inadvertently set limits on yourself and what's possible, "or better" removes them. It's that simple.

10. Be open. This is the final and trickiest step of any manifesting. Again, others have touched on it over time, but it's been less of the mainstream focus on the power of manifesting than the other elements, though I think it might be the most important.

You need to be receptive to what comes. Perhaps it's best to envision it like this:

If manifesting is akin to having your hands held together in prayer, if you keep them that way—always asking—they're never open to receive. You have to open your hands to be ready to receive.

In other words, say the prayer and then let go, leaving yourself open to what comes. That's the hard part.

Sometimes, when we're so focused on what we want or desire, we neglect to see that we have something we need right in front of us, waiting for us to pick it up. In this final step, you have to be willing to allow the Universe to provide what is best for you, and trust that it's probably better (in the long run) than what you could have imagined, especially if you've employed guideline 9.

That's the final step: Be open.

So, to summarize: create your manifestation, use it, hold the image in your mind, feel the outcome in your body, and then release it all to the Universe, opening yourself to the reply that comes back.

Those are the guidelines for powerful manifesting and creating the life you desire. Keep this in mind as we progress deeper into the different scenarios. For your convenience, here are the guidelines again, in list format:

1. **Start small.**
2. **Write it down.**
3. **Use action words.**
4. **Use the positive expression of a word.**
5. **Take ownership.**
6. **Be consistent and repetitive.**
7. **Use visualization.**
8. **Feelings matter.**
9. **"Or better."**
10. **Be open.**

Additionally, to make it easier as you move through the chapters, I've created a bookmark with the guidelines that you can download from my website (www.martinafaulkner.com). I hope it helps.

Now, let's flip the proverbial coin over and look at the other side of manifesting to gain a little perspective.

CHAPTER 4

A Little Perspective

"Not enough people in this world, I think,
carry a cosmic perspective with them.
It could be life-changing."

— *Neil deGrasse Tyson* —

Before we dive into creating your manifesting phrases, we need to start with the Universal Laws, a few disclaimers, caveats, and other thoughts.

Red Flags and Warnings

To begin with, there are warning signs on the roadside of life. Did you know? These are the little flags that pop up as we go along, alerting us to obstacles or danger ahead, sometimes right where we're standing.

As a life coach, part of my job is to have a giraffe-like neck that can see a little bit ahead of where you are and raise awareness to these signs. Once I spot them and we agree that they are indeed there, you are able to make more informed decisions. Which, after all is said and done, is the ultimate goal: to make the best decisions we can at any given moment, for our greater good, and the greater good of those around us.

Road signs come in all different shapes, colors, and sizes. No two are alike. In fact, the same exact sign can show up differently for two different people or show up differently for the same person at a different time. Actually, it almost always does. Therefore, these warnings can be a challenge to spot as we're going along.

Luckily, though, there are a few tricks that you can use to spot these signs when you are working on change. Because even if they look different, warnings have some things in common: They all require us to "buy in" to something at some point.

What do I mean by "buying in?"

In order to buy into something, we have to agree with it on some level, even if we don't. Contradictory, I know. Simply stated:

When we can reason our way into agreement, even partially, we can accept it (even partially) and then buy into it.

You've heard the phrase, "I'm not buying it," right? If, eventually, that person changes their mind, something had to happen to cause them to do so. That "something" was comprised of reasoning. So, the warning signs involve reasoning, such as: rationalization, justification, explanation, generalization, and judgment.

Let's look at each one of these for a moment and see how it shows up to get us into agreement with it, and often out of alignment with our values.

Rationalization is the process by which you talk yourself into something through progressive thought. It's how you can get from A to Z in individual steps. With each step, each statement brings A and Z closer together. Alone, they don't match up and never will. Once they're linked through the 24 remaining steps, suddenly it's easy to relate Z back to A, and it somehow makes sense. When we engage in rationalization, we are actually circumventing our intuition and/or our knowledge.

For example, a person can go from thinking it's crazy to spend $500 on a wallet, to believing $495 is a bargain. This is a true story from my personal history involving progressive rationalization that also incorporated justification after the fact.

Rationalization requires baby steps, such as a $50 or $100 wallet, followed by a $225 wallet. A while later it becomes a $375 wallet, eventually resulting in a $495 wallet. It takes time and steps, but ultimately it can happen. A wallet may seem ridiculous, but it's one of the more benign ways that rationalization can wreak havoc.

The process also requires a little bit of external input, in that there must be some external measurement or pressure that extols the virtues and benefits of a $500 wallet. In my case, it was the "hype" of a sale. Again, there's a buy-in that occurs over time and results in rationalization along the way.

Justification is a little different. Justification is rationalization in hindsight. The decision has already been made, and usually the action has been taken. Then there's an outcome that we may not have expected, or that someone in our sphere has reacted to. Enter justification. It's a way out of feeling accountable and sometimes used to avoid consequences.

To use the wallet example again, the perfect justification for me was to say "but it was on sale." Anything that supports the original decision as a wise—and even healthy—one is a justification.

Similar to justification, **Explanation** involves hindsight and a re-jiggering of facts; it's the argument side of justification. Where justification is more of a focus on the self, and often a dialogue with the self, explanation is an externalized endeavor that often involves blame.

Here we see a variation of the "on sale" argument, but it is attached to something external. In this scenario, the explanation might be something like, "Well, since you spent $800 on a camera lens, $495 on a wallet seemed like nothing."

Justification and explanation are very similar and often interchangeable. What distinguishes them from each other is the interpersonal action inherent in the statement. Justification is often a bit more internalized. Whereas explanation involves defending yourself to someone else.

Generalization is the ultimate distraction tool. If you don't want the spotlight on yourself, the best thing to do is to swing it around toward the audience. That's what generalization does. It's the "ultimate" because it just doesn't get bigger than this.

When all else fails, converting your thinking into statements that are applicable to the general population is a way out of being held accountable for any decisions or actions. It's the Lemming Principal (i.e.

if everyone else has done it, you're just choosing to go with the flow or not rock the boat).

Furthermore, it becomes much easier to engage in irrational behavior when the group mentality supports your own. It may seem silly, but it's not. Back to the wallet: It is much easier to spend $495 on a wallet when your environment supports this type of decision. It's also easier to deflect any accountability for a bad decision when it's the "norm." Generalization may seem somewhat benign. The truth is it's anything but.

Finally, there's **judgment**. Judgment is also a distraction tool that creates an external focus. Judgment is poison to both parties, but more so to the one practicing judgment. *(I wrote a piece on this in my blog, which you can find here: http://bit.ly/1DQ2g0n)*

Judgment is what happens when we're feeling somehow challenged internally. Judgment is an external expression of internal discomfort. I could go into all the related challenges and issues that judgment creates, but it really all leads to one place: Judgment damages ourselves and others.

Again, this list is not exhaustive. There are many more warning signs on the roadside of life, but this is a good place to start. Now, let's ask a more important question: How do you use this knowledge?

Awareness is a prerequisite for change.

If you are engaging in any of these behaviors (and we all do), you would do well to consider it as a red flag. Usually it means that something else is going on underneath. See if you can take a moment to pause and redirect yourself out of the behavior. Alternatively, you can take note of what is triggering you into this reaction so that you can begin to understand your patterns.

These behavioral warning signs show up when we are out of personal alignment. In relation to manifesting, we need to manifest from a place of authenticity in order to be effective. If we are engaging in any of these practices of reasoning, we probably aren't being authentic, and it's an opportunity for us to realign to our true self. It's a personal and singular process.

There's another warning sign, however, that pertains to others and involves the wrong use of will.

Imposing your will on others—I would argue—is indeed the biggest warning sign there is.

Okay, so here's the deal:

You cannot manifest something bad to happen to someone else.

Well, you can, or at least you can try, but just like manifesting all the good awesome things, if you try to manifest ill on someone by focusing on all that negative energy, guess what comes back to you? It's really quite simple: If it's not kind, don't do it. It's always a better decision to remain neutral than to wish harm.

It doesn't matter if it's an invocation, a manifestation, an affirmation, a prayer, a hope, or a wish. Wishing ill on someone is simply wrong and entirely out of alignment with the Universe and everything you are. You know this to be true. Deep in your heart you will hear that small voice nodding in agreement with what I just said.

Now, this doesn't mean you don't have your feelings. People do all sorts of things to other people for various reasons, and a lot of it isn't nice. It also hurts. What I am saying is: It's okay to hurt. It's healthy to hurt if you've been hurt. Allow yourself to feel what you feel. If you feel hurt, then hurt. Cry. Yell. Scream. Whatever it takes to help yourself through the emotion of the hurt. Just don't layer onto it any sort of retribution. The Universe doesn't look kindly on that. So, if you find yourself doing it—it's time to take a big pause. Breathe. Find your heart again—even if it hurts. Especially if it hurts. Then breathe some more.

This isn't altruistic mumbo jumbo, by the way. This is a simple truth.

What you think and what you do breeds more of the same.

If you project negative thoughts onto someone else — you will eventually receive negative things. Simple. It's the Law of Attraction at work. So, if you want a happy, blessed, loving life, just don't wish the opposite for someone else, no matter what they did to you. Which brings us back to imposing on others and their free will.

I can't state this enough: Free will trumps all.

It's the whole *Love Potion #9* issue. You can't manifest someone into loving you. You can, however, manifest the opportunities you need to find and meet someone who will love you completely, as you will love them. But, if you're focused on Mr. Smith, and Mr. Smith isn't focused on you, you cannot manifest Mr. Smith into loving or marrying you. And if, by some chance you do, in the end it probably won't work because you've imposed on somebody else's free will.

This comes up often in issues of love, but it also comes up in issues of family, perhaps even more. Here's an example:

Let's say your father wants you to become an accountant. And, for the sake of argument, let's say you hate numbers and anything to do with accounting. Your father could be the most enlightened person in the world, meditating daily, maintaining a healthy spiritual practice, eating well to support his body and his mind, and yet, he still believes he knows best and wants you to become an accountant, because he's one... or perhaps because he isn't.

Either way, if he wants to manifest something for you based on his own knowledge, perception, filters, and experience, he can't. At the end of the day, he doesn't have the power to manifest for you. He only has the power to manifest opportunities that (he hopes) will steer you in the direction he desires for you. Maybe.

It's important to realize this truth. Nobody can manifest you into something you don't wish to do or be. You have free will. And the converse is true. If you're the parent in that example, you cannot manifest your child into a career or relationship, or anything. You can manifest opportunities for them to realize their highest potential for their greatest good. That is all. Trying to do more is... well, it's imposing.

And while we're on the subject, here's the last warning sign with regard to manifesting:

If it's not meant to be, you can't manifest it into being.

Ouch!

Ok, so it's not necessarily a "warning sign" as much as it is a Universal truth that we all need to accept. If it's not meant to be, you can't manifest it... sort of. There are always exceptions to the rule, and free will has a big role to play when that happens.

The best example I can think of to demonstrate this is when a spiritual teacher of mine said to me regarding a challenging relationship I was in, "Well, you can 'choose' him, even though it's not best for you. You have that power." The relationship wasn't "meant to be" long-term, but I had a choice. I could trump what was "meant to be" by exercising my free will. I could have created a longer relationship. I could have dug my heels in and chosen something other than what was happening, or what the Universe was offering. I have free will.

But here's my thinking on that: if it's not meant to be, why would you want to force it? Because if you do, you're cutting yourself off from something that *is* meant to be, and would most likely be better than you can imagine.

This is a difficult one to swallow. Trust me, I know. After everything I've just written, I know this is the last thing you want to hear. I get it. And I'm sorry, but it's true.

You may feel like shutting the book at this point, and I would understand that feeling, but I'm going to ask you to continue. Why? Because I speak from experience on this, and I'm glad.

Why would I be glad that I was unable to manifest something I deeply desired and thought I wanted? For the same reason that we include guideline 9: "Or Better." If I had received what I had asked for, "better" would never have been able to come along.

Let me say that again for emphasis:

If I had received what I had asked for, better would never have been able to come along.

What's most important here is to realize that some-times we don't know what's best for us, even when we're convinced we do.

In some circles this is the equivalent of "letting go and letting God." (There's even a Garth Brooks song about *Unanswered Prayers* that reiterates this very sentiment.) Which brings us full circle back to the guidelines on manifesting: Know yourself, do your best, and then let it go. Trust that the Universe has got your back and might (just might) know better than you.

I did just that myself, and though it took some time (and repeat performances), I learned the importance of trusting the Universe. Here's another example from my own life:

There was a time when I was transitioning from corporate America to self-employment, somewhat unwillingly. At the time, life had crashed around me. My father had gotten sick, and I chose to leave my stable corporate job and move back home with my (now ex-) husband to help my parents. Initially, my company was awesome. They set me up with a home office and allowed me to work at odd hours, which enabled me to help out around the house and assist my parents in their transition. I managed to maintain my job for about 5 or 6 months, until it became clear that it wasn't the best solution... for the company. It was great for me, actually.

I prayed, and manifested, and prayed more. I begged the Universe to allow me to keep my job, because the truth was, I loved it. I had found something that I was really good at that I enjoyed. Plus I was at the beginning of what could have been a very fun and lucrative career. Why wouldn't I want to stay?

The Universe had other plans. All my manifesting and praying left me with nothing. No matter what I did, I couldn't "make" it happen for myself. One to two years later, after things had settled down at home, I tried to get back into the same industry with a different company, to no avail. I prayed and manifested, and by then I had a much greater understanding of what that all meant because I had begun to study Reiki and work with the spiritual laws on a regular basis. And still nothing happened. There was no job offer, no renewal of my career.

Years later I understood why. I was blocked at every turn by the Universe, because returning to my corporate career wasn't my path. And wow, am I grateful! Had I received my request and my manifesting resulted in the outcome I desired, I wouldn't be here writing this book and helping others transform their lives. Maybe I would in another 10 or 20 years, but not today. I wouldn't be helping others, and I wouldn't have rediscovered myself or reconnected to my authenticity and my inner power. I would have been a very different version of who I am, and I would have delayed finding my true calling and purpose in life. And that would have been a shame.

Thankfully, the Universe knew better. Now I know how important it is to let them do their job after I've done my part.

And that's it. That's the simple truth of manifesting: **Do your part, and then let the Universe do its job.**

Manifesting and being open to the Power of Possibility isn't rocket science. It's not some miraculous power only a select few possess. If you follow the guidelines and understand the basic rules of the Universe, manifesting change for your life is within your grasp. It's within everyone's grasp. All you have to do is start. And remember:

When you let go of expectations, you open yourself to possibility.

So I ask you:

What if.. anything were possible?

What if.. your dreams could come true?

CHAPTER 5

Identifying Your Dreams

"It's the possibility of having a dream come true that makes life interesting."

— *Paulo Coelho* —

What would you ask for **if** you could?

We have all been taught and/or told that we are supposed to live in the present, in the now. But fully living in the present is usually a byproduct of something else we're doing. Living in the present is the happy consequence of understandings we have put into practice on a consistent and deliberate basis. It's the byproduct of doing our work in alignment with who we are.

Now, **What if** you could contribute to the script of your life as it's being written? **What if** you had the power to create your life? **What if** you could impact the outcomes?

What if..?

You're only limited by your own beliefs. What you hold to be true will always impact your ability to manifest and create the life you desire and need. So, we have to start there.

What do you believe?

- About yourself?
- About others?
- About society?
- About culture?
- About life?

Basically, the question to ask is:

What do you believe and how have those beliefs impacted your life?

It's time to take a mini-inventory of your life and understand where you're starting, so you can begin to plan the course for where you want to go.

How do you do this? By answering the questions above and a few others that I created to get you thinking about where you are in your life.

The Belief Questions

Beliefs do more than influence our perspective; they drive our decisions. When was the last time you made a decision without running it past some belief you hold? Here's a good example:

Let's say you have a special event to attend and you want to go out and get something new to wear. Many thought patterns — or beliefs — are going to affect the decision you make on what to buy and what to wear. You'll most likely have healthy beliefs, neutral beliefs, and unhealthy beliefs popping up and interweaving with each other like a thought-braid in your mind.

In the healthy beliefs category you might think of things like: 'I feel good in blue' or 'skirts make me feel empowered' or even 'wearing something new will give me confidence.' These are thoughts that are often supportive and always in alignment with your Self.

In the neutral beliefs category you might think something like: 'black is slimming' or 'skinny ties are more hip' or 'heels make legs look longer.' These are more likely to come from the realm of commonly held conventions that we're taught over time and are often highlighted in fashion magazines. They're not your original thoughts. They are comprised of things you've learned externally.

In the unhealthy beliefs category there might be lurking thoughts, such as: 'It doesn't matter what I wear, nobody will care and/or I'm not important enough' or perhaps 'Nothing ever fits me properly' or 'I'm too fat to wear a sexy dress.' Even 'I'm too broke to buy myself something new' can be an unhealthy belief. (Yes, your bank account may not be supportive of purchasing a new outfit, but holding onto and reinforcing that belief is holding you back in some way.)

Now, the truth of any or all of those statements lies in the realm of perspective and belief. It's all subjective. Therefore, knowing what beliefs you hold about yourself and others, as well as what beliefs you've been taught, is important to understand before you begin any enterprise of manifesting.

Our beliefs influence our language, and language is a key component in manifesting and using the Power of Possibility to change your life.

So, what are your beliefs?

The easiest way to identify them is to write down your self-talk. Make a list of your most common phrases that run around in your head. Are they about you? Your worth? Are they about others? Life? Society? Limitations or possibilities? **Our self-talk is the first indicator of what we actually hold to be true, even if it's not.** Unpackaging our self-talk and laying it out on the table for examination is the first step to understanding what you believe. It's time to go get your notebook and start writing.

This might actually be an uncomfortable exercise for many of you. It was for me. When I actually started listening to my thoughts, I was somewhat shocked by what I heard. Like elevator music running in the background of my life, my thoughts were a constant stream of input, and they weren't all healthy.

Ok, truth time: When I started my wellness journey most were unhealthy, actually. I had a lot of negative thought patterns to unpack, examine, and make decisions about. It was depressing and uncomfortable. But, most worthwhile journeys begin with a little uncertainty and discomfort. It may, or may not, be the same for you.

What I know is that anything is possible when you're willing to take pause, look in the mirror, and be present with yourself without judgment.

If that journaling exercise is a bit difficult or not structured enough, here are some questions/scenarios to get you thinking about your existing beliefs and thought patterns in a less intensive way. Do as many or as few as you wish.

1. You see a homeless person sitting on the ground with an empty cup, asking for money. What is your first thought?

2. You see a person walking in front of you who is wearing skinny jeans, a leather jacket, has long hair that looks unwashed, and is playing loud music on their phone without headphones. What assumptions are you making?

3. You have a big important meeting at work, your morning has not gone well at home, and now you've spilled coffee on your shirt 30 minutes before the meeting. What do you say to yourself?

4. Your partner (or friend) is sad and won't share with you what's going on in their mind. What are you thinking about them, and about yourself?

5. You're in the supermarket and watch a woman get her child's attention by tugging on his/her hair. What story are you telling yourself? What if it were the child tugging the woman's hair?

6. What do you believe about God? What religion(s) were you raised with, if any?

7. What stories interest you the most on the evening news? What do you listen to?

8. If you are on social media, and you share quotes, articles, or stories, what types of items do you share? Why?

9. When something goes wrong or poorly in your life, despite your best intentions, what do you say to yourself and others?

10. Do you believe people are genuinely doing the best they are capable of in any given moment? Or do you believe that they could always be doing better?

The last question was asked on the first day of class by my grad school professor, Brené Brown. It stuck with me, and I imagine it always will. Because, as she said: You can't believe both of those statements at the same time. You are either in one camp, or another. Interestingly, when she asked the first part, most of the class raised their hands in agreement. Then she asked the second part, and over half of the hands were still raised.

It was only in explaining the basis of the concept that it became clear what she was teaching. This was my take-away from that morning:

Hindsight often makes us judge and jury of ourselves and others. But decisions in any given moment are made without the benefit of hindsight. So if you believe people are genuinely doing the best they can in any given moment, it's not possible for someone to do better than they did.

Did you get that? It's a simple concept that can be challenging to grasp and even more difficult to fully accept. I encourage you to read it again and revisit it if you need to.

Now, I think you get the basic idea and have a good starting point to begin to access the mental soundtrack in your life, whether you've been aware of it or not. And, don't worry if, like me, you find that you have a plethora of unhealthy belief systems. That just means that you have a whole lot of mental real estate that is about to become available for some really awesome and healthy ones.

∞

Once you have a deeper understanding of what you believe and hold to be true, you can begin to assess its value in your life. You see, sometimes we hold something to be true without ever cross-checking it with our values. In those instances, we are living out of alignment with who we are.

It's important to know and understand what we believe, but it's perhaps even more important to know our values. Next is a values exercise that you can go through to help you better understand yourself and prioritize your goals.

The Values Exercise

Below is a short list of commonly identified values. This list is a compilation of those I have used from various sources. I first heard a variation of the values exercise during my coaching certification training. Since then, I have seen it used with great success across multiple programs and specializations.

(There are numerous resources on the web for this exercise. If you'd like a more extensive list, it's just a Google search away. Type in "values list" and you will receive over 665 million results with a lot of overlap. Any will do. A caution here: the longer the list, the harder and more overwhelming the exercise. I've created a shortened list of 40 to allow for ease of completion.)

Now, here's my slightly different take on the exercise. I think we live in our heads too much, and as such we don't often get accurate results when we think our way through a list like this. So I created a way to engage the mind a little less, and engage the intuition a little more. (I do this exercise as a stand-alone workshop, and it's powerful. If it helps, ask a friend to conduct it for you, or do it for each other.)

To do the exercise, you first need to get clear. Take some deep breaths, then scan the list quickly and highlight the values that stand out for you the most on this first pass. Take a 5-minute break and do something fun, like listen to your favorite song. Then, on a clean piece of paper with only the things you highlighted listed, repeat that first step, narrowing it down to 8–10 values. Take note if a word pops into your mind that you don't see listed.

Once you have your list of 8–10 values, repeat the exercise once more by circling your top five, and write them down in the journal you've created for this work.

Now you have the five most important values by which you live written down in black and white. You can prioritize your life and your goals from this perspective.

Here is the shortened values list you can use to conduct this exercise. Start with the question: What do you value most?

Acceptance
Accountability
Appreciation
Attractiveness
Authenticity
Career
Commitment
Compassion
Courage
Creativity
Duty
Education
Empathy
Equality
Ethics
Faith
Family
Freedom
Gratitude
Honesty

Hope
Humility
Humor
Integrity
Joy
Kindness
Leadership
Love
Loyalty
Patience
Respect
Responsibility
Self-respect
Service
Spirituality
Stability
Tradition
Trust
Wealth
Wisdom

∞

Pulling it all together

You've just completed two exercises that give you a baseline understanding of your beliefs and your values. This means you have a deeper knowledge of what you believe, and you now also know what your priorities are for your life. It's from this position that we can begin to outline and manifest your future using the **What if..?** model.

A question might come up at this point: what exactly are you trying to do when manifesting? It can be a scary thought, actually. Giving someone permission to exercise their power can be daunting for a lot of people: "What if I screw up?" "What if I ask for the wrong things?" "What if I can't do this?" (Did you see all the negative "What ifs" in there?)

These are just some of the thoughts that could be running around your head. It's exciting and terrifying to know that we are the co-creators of our own lives. It's a big responsibility. The truth is, though, you've already been doing it. Now, you're just going to do it deliberately with more discernment and (hopefully) joy!

Manifesting is all about seeding your reality.

Still a little unsure what you're doing when you're manifesting for your future? Well, here's one way you can look at it: You're seeding your reality. You're planting seeds in the garden of your life, so that you can reap the harvest at some point in the future. This is why manifesting isn't a one-time deal. This is why manifesting becomes a part of your daily life once you start doing it.

What do I mean by that?

When you plant a garden, you don't plant one seed, focus intensely on it, baby it, and sit next to it praying for it to take root. You don't depend on one seed to provide you with sustenance or beauty for a lifetime. No, you plant many seeds. You spread them out, follow the directions for planting (or not), and do your best, leaving the rest up to nature.

Manifesting is exactly the same. You plant lots of seeds, deliberately. Then you allow nature (the Universe) to take its course, trusting that it knows best and works effectively and efficiently.

You're the gardener of your life. Decide what kind of garden you want and need to sustain you emotionally, physically, mentally, and spiritually; pick your seeds; and start planting.

∞

Ten chapters follow, each on a common area of manifestation, each of which explores the application and understanding of **What if..?** as a tool for manifesting. The chapters are not meant to be all-inclusive. Rather, they take each issue in turn, using the same formula for tapping into the Power of Possibility.

You can read the chapters in order or jump to the one that speaks to you the most. Each chapter begins with a list of questions to get you thinking. You do not need to answer every question. How you use the book is up to you. The questions are there to serve as a guide and to stimulate thought.

Similarly, each chapter has examples and exercises to promote depth of understanding for the **What if..?** concept. The examples are meant to serve as anecdotes and are not exhaustive. If a specific example does not work for you, do your best to come up with your own scenario in order to make the exercise come to life.

For example, if the section on sexual expression doesn't apply to you, change it to emotional expression or artistic expression instead. Similarly, if you don't dream of winning the lottery, change "lottery" to whatever it is you dream of regularly. It's your choice. Get creative and personalize each scenario to meet your specific needs.

As I've mentioned, there is no "right" or "wrong" way to use this book. At this point, we are beginning a process that can be fun, engaging, and exciting. If it feels overwhelming or discouraging, take a break, step away, and pause. Reconnect with what makes your heart smile. Take a walk, play with your kids, listen to music. Anything that will get your heart back online is a good thing.

As with everything, what matters most is that you are staying true to yourself, acting in accordance with your core values, and staying in alignment with who you are. Remember, this is meant to be expansive and fun.

Sure, making change is a serious business, but that doesn't mean it can't also be fun! In fact, in my experience, the more fun I'm having, the more likely I am to do it again. I see it all the time in my workshops —the more creative and fun experiences lead to the greatest commitment to exploration and change.

Daydreaming is joy-filled. Allow yourself to experience the joy of creativity and creation. And then make a point of finding something joyful to do.

As I've said before: use the book. Only you can decide how that works for you. And once again, happy daydreaming!

Here we go!

CHAPTER 6

On Self-Love

"To love oneself is the beginning
of a life-long romance."

— *Oscar Wilde* —

What if..

You fell in love with yourself?

Let's start by answering a few questions. At the beginning of this and subsequent chapters, I will pose a series of questions to get you more connected with yourself. The goal is not to answer every question. Pick a couple that jump out at you and focus on those, knowing you can return to this chapter at a later date and look at other questions if you want to do more in-depth work. *(Because I suggest using this book rather than reading it, I'll also add this little reminder at the beginning of each of the following chapters for your convenience.)*

Questions to get you thinking (pick one or two):

- How would your life be different if you loved yourself?

- What would change if you woke up each morning with someone you love and went to bed each night with that same person?

- What if this someone loved you back, unconditionally and always?

- How would it feel to know that there is always someone there for you who loves you and supports you, believes in you, and shares your hopes and dreams?

Questions to get you feeling and seeing (pick one or two):

- Would you walk differently?
- Dress differently?
- Speak differently?

- How would you show up at family gatherings? Or work meetings?
- What kind of language would you use with those around you to share and express who you are ?
- What would it mean to you to know you are loved completely?

At this point, we've heard from enough teachers, authors, gurus, thought leaders, spiritualists, and many, many others on the importance of loving ourselves. We've learned that we can't truly love someone else unless we love ourselves first. But is that true?

Yes. And no. (Not the answer you wanted, right? Sorry about that.) Let me break it down.

Yes, you can love others if you don't love yourself first. I know this from personal experience. I loved many other people while struggling to love myself. My lack of self-love didn't prevent me from loving others. And my discovery of self-love didn't suddenly make me a miraculous lover walking around offering hugs, love and light to everyone I met. (Can you imagine?)

Self-love gave me a different perspective on what it meant to give and receive love, and it is ever-evolving as I grow and progress. It isn't necessarily "better" or "worse;" it's different. It's as if I know more, and in knowing more I am able to share more of myself. The main difference then, for me, was an understanding of love.

I explain it like this: Loving others without self-love is a bit like giving a lecture on a topic with all of your notes coming from one or two sources. It's good, it's informative, it's not false, and it certainly can hit the mark.

Whereas loving others from a place of self-love is like giving the same lecture with the resources from all the libraries in the world available to you. Your notes will probably change, your information will most likely be a bit more well-rounded, and your presentation will be richer for it.

There's a wisdom that comes from self-love that isn't learned any other way.

That's the reason, I feel, we've seen the push for self-love as a primary goal. That's the reason behind the movement. Self-love gives us access to knowing love on a very personal level, and it's from that space that we are able to share our love more fully.

At its core, self-love is a Self-ish act. It's my opinion that being Self-ish is a good thing. It means you're willing to take care of yourself, invest in yourself, and respect yourself. It's not the same as being self-centered, arrogant, or narcissistic. When it's healthy, in balance, and aligned with Self, being Self-ish can be a very positive thing.

When we're talking about self-love, we're not talking about self-absorption or self-centeredness. Those are very important distinctions to make.

Self-love is about honoring yourself, respecting yourself, and taking care of yourself. It's about treating yourself the way you deserve to be treated. Truly deserve, not some idea of what you think you're worth or not worth based on some external measurement. *(This is where the work on beliefs and values that we've already done comes into play.)*

We are all deserving of love, respect, honor, and wellness. That's a universal truth. Self-love is an expression of that, from you to you. Furthermore, it's an announcement to the Universe that you know you are deserving of those things.

Self-absorption and self-centeredness are pretty much the opposite of self-love. In my experience, they are usually indicative of a low level of self-esteem. They tend to be defense mechanisms used to protect an inner core of insecurity or fear. Even though this person is focused on themselves, it's a surface level focus or an externalized self-focus. It's about them in relation to the world, not them in relation to themselves. This is why it's defensive. Like a good fortress, it's shielding the inner core.

When we feel insecure or scared, we may have a tendency to act out more, blaming and shaming others for our shortcomings or challenging situations and decisions — especially if they've gone awry.

When we love ourselves and practice self-love, our presence becomes more of a gift to those around us. We create and keep healthy boundaries. We respect others' decisions and paths in life, and we work hard to keep ourselves healthy and in balance. We model healthy behavior for others who might be struggling. In many ways, we become a beacon of hope, possibility, and joy. Effortlessly.

You can think of it like this:

At the end of the day, whether you share your life with others or not, you always share your life with one person: You.

You are the person you spend the most time with, eating meals, thinking, laughing, and loving. You are your best friend and truest companion. You sleep with yourself every night and wake up with yourself every morning. You are the one person who is always there for you, no matter what. You show up, do your best, and you can't ask for more than that. Therefore, if you're willing to love someone else who isn't even capable of doing all these things for you, why wouldn't you also love yourself?

As I have said, there is love without self-love. It's possible. It's even probable. But love is made even better when you add self-love into the mix.

How does this work in manifesting greater self-love? Here are some **What if..?** phrases you can try out to get started:

What if I loved myself?

What if I chose to love myself?

What if I fell in love with myself?

What if I loved myself enough to treat myself well, with respect and joy, and asked others to do the same?

What if loving myself became a standard by which I invited others to love me, and **What if** that standard was always growing with greater love and respect for myself?

What if I loved myself enough to allow myself to make mistakes, live openly, feel my emotions, and know that I was always safe, cherished, and whole, exactly as I am at any given moment, because I loved myself?

How would your life be different? How would it be the same? Can you begin to imagine it? I can. It feels quite beautiful.

CHAPTER 7

On Relationships

"The meeting of two personalities is like the contact of two chemical substances: if there is any reaction, both are transformed."

— C.G. Jung —

What if..

You created strong, healthy, and fulfilling relationships?

Reminder: Let's start by answering a few questions to get you more connected with yourself. The goal is

not to answer every question. Pick a couple that jump out at you and focus on those, knowing you can return to this chapter at a later date and look at other questions if you want to do more in-depth work.

Questions to get you thinking (pick one or two):

- How would your life be different if you had healthier relationships with the people around you?
- What would change about your interactions with your loved ones?
- How would you treat yourself differently? How would you allow yourself to be treated? And how would you treat others?
- What is involved in healthy relationships?
- How would it feel to know your relationships are at their best?

Questions to get you feeling and seeing (pick one or two):

- What does a healthy relationship look like? Feel like? What does it mean?
- Would you laugh more? Smile more?
- How would you express yourself differently?
- What activities would you engage in?

Let's start by reiterating that you can't impose your will on anybody else. We all have free will for a reason, so you can't "manifest" somebody to be with you who does not choose to be with you. As I've said, this isn't *Love Potion #9*.

This is about exercising and leveraging the Power of Possibility to live the best life you can live. If somebody else joins you and shares in that joy — wonderful! Bottom line: We can't change others; we can only change ourselves. I know you know that, but sometimes it helps to have reminders.

Now that the disclaimer is out of the way, let's get on to manifesting the best possible relationships you can have. We're talking about all types of relationships here, not just the romantic ones. Parent/child, boss/employee, friends, relatives — they're all relationships. Additionally, we've already talked about self-love, so this isn't about your relationship with yourself. This is about empowering you to visualize what "healthy" and "strong" look like for you in your relationships with others. Sometimes that means stronger boundaries, sometimes that means prioritizing values. Actually, it usually means both.

Hands down, one of the most-often addressed issues in coaching and therapy is that of interpersonal relationships. Even in my Reiki practice, the majority of time was spent working on the energy surrounding relationships and how that is stored in the body. Relationships seem to be our number one area of concern when we seek out supportive services. Why? Because relationships make up, drive, and define so much of who we are.

Think about it this way: If I were to ask you who you were, how would you answer me? Would you say, I'm:

a mother, a daughter, a parent, a spouse, a partner, a child, a sister, a brother, a husband, an uncle, a grandparent, a friend, a lover.

Or would you say: I'm me.

Typically, we define ourselves using our identities based on what we are in relation to somebody else. Our first response might also be more centered on what we do, such as "I'm a lawyer" or "I'm a stay-at-home mom." In a few cases this overlaps, such as "I'm a student." This statement clearly defines what I'm doing (studying) as well as my relationship to others (classmates/teachers).

Recently I told a friend, "I'm a great aunt." *(Not "great" as in two generations older, but great as in "awesome." Yes, I believe I am, but you can ask my nieces and nephew for verification.)* After that conversation, I realized how clearly I had defined myself through a single relationship in just a few short words.

The first step to manifesting better relationships is to identify how you define yourself.

The second step is to ask yourself: Am I limiting myself by this definition? What would I change, if anything?

In each instance you may have a different response to what you would change. In fact, it's highly likely that you will, and that's okay. That's good because each relationship is different and therefore should be handled differently.

When it comes to manifesting a better relationship with someone, it's all about **how you choose to show up and how you allow yourself to be treated.** We could go back several millennia and reiterate the golden rule:

Do unto others as you would have them do unto you.

Well, that's mostly true. When it comes to respect, it's an absolute must (remember, no imposing your will on somebody else). When it comes to behaviors and actions, it's partly true. Here's why:

Sometimes, we treat others better than we treat ourselves, or allow ourselves to be treated. *(A-ha!)*

Both instances imply that we aren't being treated very well. If you're treating others well, it follows that they should treat you well. The hiccup is that we can't control anybody else, so the rule starts to break down. Furthermore, if we're treating others as we wish to be treated and we're not treating ourselves very well, that's akin to giving others permission to not treat us very well either. So, the rule breaks down a bit more. Perhaps it's better to revise Confucius a little and think of it like this:

Do your best—for yourself and others—always.

This removes the issue of controlling someone else or placing expectations on outcomes. It removes them from the equation except as a recipient of your kindness, respect, and love. This is a much healthier way to go about engaging in a relationship. It doesn't mean, however, that you put up with anything and everything. This is where boundaries come in.

Boundaries are the greatest gift you can give to yourself and someone else. Should I say that last part again?

Boundaries are the greatest gift you can give to yourself and someone else.

Think about it for a second. Boundaries are like having a written manual about you that you give to someone else. They don't have to spend all that time guessing and trying to figure out what you need or how to treat you. You've made it clear up front, and they are free to enjoy your relationship without all the muckety-muck of second-guessing and assumption-making. What a gift! Let the healthy relationships begin!

Which brings us back to the bigger question: How do you use the **What if..?** to manifest or empower healthier relationships with others?

Well, **What if** you used it to empower yourself? What does that look like?

Here's an example I've used before:

What if.. I showed up honestly and completely in each interaction I have with my friend while maintaining my boundaries and authenticity?

Okay, so that's more of the big picture or theoretical **What if..?** example. Let's try a simpler one.

Recently I've seen a lot of articles on the lack of interpersonal communication due to the excessive use of smartphones. I've witnessed it myself as I've been out and about. The majority of people I see are walking around face-in-screen, hardly interacting with one another. So, let's try that one on for size:

What if.. every time I was with a friend I chose to silence my phone and put it away, and I asked her/him to do the same?

How does that feel? That's an example that uses boundaries as well as an emphasis on one's values in order to arrive at a healthier relationship. We can take it a step further, too.

What if.. every time I was with a friend I chose to put away my phone, asked them to do the same, and made a point of looking them in the eye while listening to them as they spoke, allowing myself to be fully present with them in that moment, without judgment or simultaneously crafting a reply to their words? **What if..** I truly listened as they were speaking and they did the same in return for me?

This is what it means to open the door to the Power of Possibility. This is what it looks like to empower yourself in your interactions, thereby building stronger, healthier relationships.

Each time you write a phrase, you get an idea to make it better, more powerful. With each pass your manifesting gets clearer, and you open the door to even greater potential.

As always, the choice is yours to craft the **What if..?** phrase that best suits your needs, and then use the guidelines outlined at the beginning of the book to visualize and feel the results of each moment of manifesting. Just remember that manifesting improved relationships is never about changing someone else. It's always about changing how you show up in relation to someone else.

CHAPTER 8

On Companionship

"The trouble is not that I am single and likely to stay single, but that I am lonely and likely to stay lonely."

— *Charlotte Brontë* —

What if..

You met your Soul Mate?

Reminder: Let's start by answering a few questions to get you more connected with yourself. The goal is not to answer every question. Pick a couple that jump

out at you and focus on those, knowing you can return to this chapter at a later date and look at other questions if you want to do more in-depth work.

Questions to get you thinking (pick one or two):
- What does the phrase "Soul Mate" mean to you?
- What is missing in your life that you think meeting your Soul Mate will fix or resolve?
- What qualities do you want in your Soul Mate?
- How would your life be different if/when you met?
- Why is it important to you to meet this person?

Questions to get you feeling and seeing (pick one or two):
- How would it feel to share your life with someone?
- What changes would you make in your daily routine?
- What activities would you enjoy together?
- What foods would you eat together?
- How do you see yourself when you're sitting next to this person?

This is one of the hottest topics to address, so of course I couldn't leave it out. When it comes to manifesting, in my experience, the top two areas of concern are money and love. So, it's time to talk about Soul Mates.

There is so much information 'out there' about Soul Mates that it's hard to discern what's true and what's not. Unfortunately, I don't think there is one truth when it comes to Soul Mates. What I do believe, however, is that anything based in fear is not a good path to explore. That means that if something or someone is suggesting that you're running out of time to find a Soul Mate or creates some urgency around the issue for you, it might be time to walk away from that source. Just a suggestion, but it usually rings true in most cases, and not just on the issue of Soul Mates.

Fear—or lack-based thinking—carries an unnecessary energy of urgency, creating a false sense of importance.

So, let's ask the obvious question: **What if** you found your Soul Mate?

Well, unless your Soul Mate is a party planner, fireworks are pretty much off the table. In fact, meeting your Soul Mate usually means that your soul's work is about to begin. Why? Because our Soul Mates are soul mates for a reason; they're there to bring us our issues, front and center, for us to do the work we need to do to evolve. If you don't want to do the work, or you're not ready, don't manifest your Soul Mate. Work on manifesting your Soul Twin instead.

I know that what I'm about to say may not be totally aligned with what you've heard before, but it's what I was taught, and it's what I have learned to be true through many other sources and experiences.

Here's the main difference between Soul Mates and Soul Twins:

Soul Mates are another aspect of your soul that seeks to reunite with you, so you can both learn and evolve faster together than you would if you remained apart. There is more than one Soul Mate for each person, too. We tend to recognize each other regardless of external factors, such as time, age, gender, race, nationality, etc., and we are drawn to each other, often without explanation. We can be joined together for a lifetime (or lifetimes) or for events or moments.

Timing is everything when it comes to meeting a Soul Mate. Recognizing and acknowledging the purpose in coming together is paramount. Once the main goals are achieved (i.e., you've learned what you needed to learn or experience) the relationship can end, or it can evolve into a Soul Twin relationship.

Soul Twins are the companions of a lifetime. These are the people who show up and bump along on our path with us. They share in our laughter and tears, and they typically come without judgment, lessons, or needs—other than companionship. A Soul Twin can be a best friend, a child, a sibling, and yes, a partner. As I've already mentioned, a Soul Mate can turn into a Soul Twin, but a Soul Twin rarely turns into a Soul Mate, unless they were already one to begin with.

So, that might be a new way of looking at the world and your most intimate of relationships, which prompts me to ask:

What if you hold this (new) information to be true? How does it change what you desire in a companion? How does it affect how you speak and interact with others? With yourself and your thoughts?

Whether you accept it to be true or not doesn't affect the process of manifesting; it just changes the language. Often I hear the phrase: "I want to manifest meeting my Soul Mate." My current reply is: "Are you sure?" Because when I hear someone saying they want to manifest their Soul Mate, more often than not what they're really saying is: I want to find my true companion. Therefore, in light of this distinction, and in order to avoid any confusion, let's use the phrase: true companion. *(Cue Marc Cohn's song into my head as I type, but I digress.)*

∞

Now, if you want to find your true companion, let's work with that. To begin with, you need to know what it feels like to be loved and supported because your true companion will do both, and much more. So, in order to manifest your true companion, you need to make a list, and you need to have access to feelings and images that support that list.

What goes on the list?

The qualities you respect, desire, and admire most in others. Start with your existing circles. Pick specific family members or friends that make you feel happy when you're around them. People who make you laugh on the inside AND outside. Pick 5–10 of those people, write down their names in a list, and then start to write down what it is you like about them and why they make you smile. (And by all means, smile as you're making the list!) Once you have the list—and you're smiling—it's time to write your **What if..?** statement for your true companion.

A good starting statement might look something like this:

What if.. I met a true companion who was kind, honest, and caring, who had a wicked sense of humor, loved music, aroused me, and whom I respected and enjoyed spending time with, and they felt the same about me?

Now, I can guess that someone might be thinking, "But I like blondes, can I add that?" The fear here is that by asking for something superficial, we may be manifesting superficially. It's not superficial to identify that which turns you on. In the example above I used the phrase "aroused me" because that would be a good way to work around a fear of being superficial. It's not shallow to know yourself. It's important to know yourself. It's also important to trust that the Universe knows you too and not limit yourself in your manifesting unnecessarily.

If you want to manifest a true companion, knowing yourself is the most important factor in creating your **What if..?** phrase. It's also key to know your "deal breakers" when manifesting a companion. These are the little items that immediately result in a no-go situation. Knowing these is equally as important as knowing what you desire, although you don't state them in your manifestation (remember the guidelines about language). What you use them for is to help raise your awareness as a filter for meeting people in the future.

If you are ready to manifest your true companion, do the work; make your list of qualities you admire, desire, and respect; and create your phrase from that space.

As in everything, but especially this, I wish you all the joy, love, and laughter in the world. May you find that in and with each other.

CHAPTER 9

On Body Image

*"To lose confidence in one's body is to
lose confidence in oneself."*

— Simone de Beauvoir —

What if..

You accepted yourself as you are?

Reminder: Let's start by answering a few questions to get you more connected with yourself. The goal is not to answer every question. Pick a couple that jump out at you and focus on those, knowing you can return to this chapter at a later date and look at other questions if you want to do more in-depth work.

Questions to get you thinking (pick one or two):
- What do you think about your physical body?
- What stories are you telling yourself?
- How would you change your body, if you could?
- What do you love about your body?
- How do you define strength?

Questions to get you feeling and seeing (pick one or two):
- When you wake in the morning, how do you feel?
- Where do you experience pain?
- What makes you feel invigorated and strong?
- When you look at other people's bodies that you admire, what are you looking at?
- When do you feel at your best?

This topic might be just as charged as the Soul Mate question, though perhaps it's a little more personal. Body image, or self-image, is one of those areas in which it's best to tread lightly. I'm not you, and you're not me. I wouldn't presume to know what you're feeling or experiencing, nor would I expect you to know the same for me. Therefore, I won't define "healthy" as being anything but just that: healthy. Additionally, we will address what it means to be healthy in greater depth in a later chapter. This chapter is about body image.

For example purposes though, I am going to use the word "thinner" because it's a common request when it comes to body image, and I hear it all the time in my practice.

Sometimes we can look at someone else and think, "If only I could look like him or her..." Meanwhile, that same person may be looking back at us and thinking the exact same thing. So much of this thinking is based in fear and inadequacy that it becomes a bit of a minefield to address from a place of manifesting and possibility. It's one of the easiest areas in which to slip back into negative thinking and manifesting from a "lesser-than" position. So, this may be a bit tricky, but I will do my best to break it down for you.

To begin with, in order to best access the energy behind the desire for change, it's important to know what's generating it. To do that we need to ask two clarifying questions to get at the energy behind the desire. Let's continue with the example:

1. What if you *were* thinner?
2. What if you *weren't* thinner?

Let's start with the latter.

This could mean you stayed exactly the same as you are now or grew. It's important to answer the question: **What if** you stayed exactly as you are now? Would your life change? Could your life change in meaningful ways? How does your body image relate to the life you have? What can you do (or not do) if you stay exactly as you are today?

Now, let's answer the first question. What would change in your life? How would you wake up differently? Where would you spend your energy and focus? How would your relationships with others change? What about your relationship with yourself?

Once you've looked at these questions *(and believe me, I know they're not simple passing conversations to have with yourself over a cup of coffee),* you will be better able to address the preliminary question of "**What if..** your body were different than it is now?" Or, more importantly:

What if.. you felt differently about your body than you do now?

In this example, examining your responses to these thoughts will provide you with insight into *why* you wish to change your body and what expectations you have in attaining that goal. You'll learn why you believe your life would change, and in what ways it would change. You'll also begin to understand what it is about looking different that is meaningful to you, and how the beliefs you hold about your body have influenced your actions, behaviors, and decisions.

Body image is a challenging subject and area for concern. It typically involves more mind than body. In fact, based on my own experience, body image usually comes back to issues of self-worth and self-love, coupled with chronic external stimuli extolling the "rewards" (wealth, success, happiness, love) associated with having a "perfect" body.

The truth is *(and somewhere deep inside you'll probably know this to be true as you read it),* you already have the perfect body. It's a truly amazing machine. This is why we call it a body *image* issue. It's about how we see ourselves.

The image we carry influences what we think, and vice versa. In the negative, it can become a never-ending loop of insecurity, discouragement, shame, embarrassment, etc. In the positive, it can be a source of confidence, strength, and love. This is why body image can be such a tricky subject.

Though I know each body to be perfect as it is, I'll concede that many of us would modify something about our physique given the opportunity. What I hear most often is: I want/need to lose 10 pounds.

So, let's ask again: What if you lost 10 pounds? How would your life change? What if it were 40 pounds? Or 100? What would inherently change in your life if your body changed? Would you love yourself more? Would you feel more deserving of love from others?

What I've noticed is that the number on a scale sometimes indicates how we think we should feel about our place in the world. Often, people who feel they take up too much physical space feel less entitled to own their place in the world. In fact, it can be even more acute: they can feel that they are undeserving of their place in the world. That can be equally true for a person who is considered underweight, normal, or overweight.

So body image is the issue, not weight. The number on a scale doesn't determine your capacity for self-love or love of others, nor is it a measurement of your worth. But if you have body image issues, it can be. I've known women who are a size 2 who believe they are unworthy of love because they don't look like the person on the cover of a magazine.

I have also known women who were a size 18 and were the most radiant and beautiful women I've ever met, because they loved themselves and their body exactly as it was. Yes, they may have wanted more toned arms, but that's not about not being "good enough"—that's about being "even better," stronger, and healthier than they already saw themselves.

For men, it can be a little different in how it manifests, but the premise is the same. It comes back to whether you are measuring your self worth using external factors or an internal understanding.

To carry the same example forward: I have known men who were completely paralyzed by their bodies, because they weren't fit enough or strong enough. Their muscles weren't big enough, their belt size was too big, their inseam too short, or they didn't have the "athletic" V-shaped physique. I have seen it stop men in their tracks from participating in life, both when it comes to being with someone they're interested in romantically, as well as being social with others.

Similarly, I have seen men who wouldn't describe themselves as attractive or physically captivating command the attention of entire rooms. Effortlessly. Why? Because they're comfortable in their skin. How they "see" themselves—the *image* they hold—defines how they show up in the world.

Therefore, if, like me, this is something that you have struggled with, the focus needs to shift from **What if** I weighed X pounds? to the more accurate question:

What if I felt comfortable in my skin?

Possibly followed by:

What if I loved myself completely as I am?

What if I honored my body for the joy, pleasure, and possibility it brings to me?

What if I accepted myself and made decisions supporting that belief?

What if I loved that part of myself that believes I am not a valid human if I don't fit an externalized standard of beauty?

As a result of this re-focusing, you may actually lose 10 pounds, or you may not. What matters is that you will be happier either way. You will feel more aligned with your body and all its possibility and capacity for joy and wellness.

You will feel more like you than ever before. High five!

CHAPTER 10

On Job and Career

*"Making money isn't hard in itself,
what's hard is to earn it doing something
worth devoting your life to."*

— Carlos Ruiz Zafón —

What if..

You had a better job?

Reminder: Let's start by answering a few questions to get you more connected with yourself. The goal is not to answer every question. Pick a couple that jump

out at you and focus on those, knowing you can return to this chapter at a later date and look at other questions if you want to do more in-depth work.

Questions to get you thinking (pick one or two):

- Using the magic wand idea, what job would you do tomorrow if you could? What about it do you like? Why does it excite you?
- What do you enjoy about your current job?
- How would you change your current job to make it more enjoyable?
- When you see a friend or family member happy in their work, what thoughts does it call up for you?
- When was the last time you had a meaningful conversation with yourself about your dreams and passions?
- What does success mean to you?

Questions to get you feeling and seeing (pick one or two):

- When you accomplish something at work, where do you feel it in your body? What does it feel like?
- If you could construct the 'perfect' day at work, what would it look like?

- Imagine (or remember) a great interaction with a co-worker and hold that memory in your body. Where do you feel it? What's causing you to smile? Why was this a great interaction?
- How would it feel to know all your bills and responsibilities were 100% covered by your salary, with some left over to save and enjoy?

To begin with, there are so many variations on this theme that I'd like to list a few more questions you can use than the original one at the start of this chapter. "Better job" was a more common way to ask the **What if..?** phrase about work. Here are a few others:

What if you enjoyed what you do?

What if you received better compensation for the work you do?

What if you felt appreciated, heard, and seen at work for your contributions?

What if you invested yourself in your job as much as you invest in other areas of your life?

What if you researched new jobs that were more aligned with your values?

What if you asked for more responsibility at work?

What if you allowed yourself to explore new options for your career?

What if you changed careers?

These are just a few of the phrases we can use to begin the conversation about work, and as you can see, they go in all different directions. Some are about job satisfaction; some are about compensation or career; and others are about appreciation and respect. This is where the values exercise comes in handy. Again, once you know what your value priorities are, it becomes easier to identify where you'd like to manifest change. *(Did you catch that? Let's say it again for emphasis.)*

Once you know what your value priorities are, it becomes easier to identify where you'd like to manifest change.

So, what do you want to change about your current job? It's time to make a list and focus in on what makes you feel alive.

There are so many posters, quotes, and books out there that tell us that if we do what we love, the money will follow. There are others that instruct us to follow our passions and we'll never feel like we are working. And still there are others that encourage us to dream, create, and do. These are all wonderful. They're fantastic road signs on the journey of life. They're also not always practical, at least not in the beginning as we're working to create change. *(Remember what I said earlier about not going from 0 to 100 overnight? This is what I'm talking about. In other words, don't quit your job while you're just starting to figure this all out and manifest something better.)*

Smaller, more manageable changes that we can create through manifesting are a good place to start. It's like this:

*You want to have strong **What if..?** phrases for both the short-term and long-term goals in your career.*

Once you've created them, you want to be open to the possibility of each happening at the appropriate time—and of things happening that you haven't dreamed of yet.

For the long-term ideas, dream big! The imagination is a wonderful thing, so daydream. Imagine that perfect job in that perfect company with that perfect salary. Allow yourself to go there, and then let it go. Remember, we're not going to attach to the outcome here, we're planting deliberate seeds for what feels good, and watching what grows, remaining open to receiving the bounty of what we've created. **What if** you were the CEO of Google if that would make you happy? Dream it. Say it. Be open to it. Why not?

For more short-term manifesting, though, let's look at a more tangible example.

One area of concern to entrepreneurs is the issue of a steady income. I've spoken with colleagues, friends, and clients about this concern and how to manifest entrepreneurial stability. I often hear the phrase "I've done everything, but I can't seem to convert prospects into paying clients."

In fact, there's a multi-million dollar industry built up around business coaching. I have several friends who are excellent business coaches. They share their knowledge in marketing, product development, and public relations in order to help their clients achieve greater levels of success and stability. Business coaching is in high demand, and I foresee it increasing as people become more specialized and clients become savvier.

That being said, manifesting is a tool that you can use to enhance your business on your own using the Power of Possibility. What does it look like to manifest stability in your business? It looks like more sales and more repeat sales. For you that might mean more product sales, for someone else, more clients. Regardless of what industry you're in, chances are you're selling something. Whether it's yourself, your skills and experience, your product or your company, in some way you're in sales.

First, though, let me say this: Not everyone is a potential client. It's very important to understand this truth. Know your client and your demographic. Understand them and their needs, and you're already one step ahead of the game. For example, I don't see everyone I meet as a potential reader of my books, attendee at a workshop, or client; it doesn't work that way. I do know, however, that potential clients weed themselves out, which means I don't have to. I just need to know what to look for.

Potential clients are interested in you. They want to know more about you, your work, or your product. They do this by coming up to you after events, sending an email, visiting your website, etc. Any time someone has invested their time in connecting with you, it's a sign that they are a potential client. If you're delivering a free presentation and there are people who have fallen asleep or left early, they're not your clients. Not today. Maybe not tomorrow. Maybe tomorrow. You don't know. What you do know is that the person in the front row taking notes and leaning forward as you speak is a potential client. And chances are you'd work well together. So, we take that into account in our manifesting.

How do you use manifesting to convert potential clients into repeat customers? You focus on attraction. I'll use myself as an example here.

Earlier in the book, I referred to José Stevens and how he delivered the final push I needed to sit down and write. José had asked me to manifest my future clients. I had recently moved and was starting my coaching business from scratch. Again.

I already had several clients I enjoyed working with, yet now that I was more settled, I was ready to expand. It was José that suggested the **What if..?** phrase to me, just as I had done with my clients, family, and friends during the prior few years.

Now, to gain more clients, you might think it would be good to say:

"What if I had more clients?"

And yes, that's true. It's a good phrase, but there are better. My various **What if..?** phrases progressed like this:

What if I attracted more clients?

What if I attracted more clients that I could work with well?

And finally…

What if I consistently and easily attracted more clients that I could really work with well, and who paid me?

I added the last part because payment is important as an exchange for services (we're back to energy and intention here). Furthermore, I had a tendency to do a lot of pro bono and sliding scale work, and I needed to address that. I still do pro bono work, and I most likely always will because it's one of my values to give back, but I needed to change the energy around the work I was doing, and so I needed to add that phrase for clarification.

Clarification in manifesting is important. The more detailed you can get, the more expansive your options become.

In college we used to do exercises around creativity and expansion. When we were working on a set design, the more ideas we came up with, the more ideas flew into our minds. It's why brainstorming sessions work. Once in the flow, everything flows. The key is getting into the flow by allowing your imagination to breathe a little.

So let's return to the original question about job and career: **What if** you had a different job or career? Where does your imagination take you when you think about those questions?

There is no limit on what's possible. Explore your mind, think of the possibilities, then write down your **What if..?** phrase and allow it to happen. You might be surprised.

CHAPTER 11

On Intimacy

*"It is not time or opportunity that
is to determine intimacy,
it is disposition alone."*

— Jane Austen —

What if..

**You had a more intimate relationship with your
partner?**

Reminder: Let's start by answering a few questions
to get you more connected with yourself. The goal is

not to answer every question. Pick a couple that jump out at you and focus on those, knowing you can return to this chapter at a later date and look at other questions if you want to do more in-depth work.

Questions to get you thinking (pick one or two):
- What does 'intimacy' mean to you?
- When you have been at your most intimate, what were the circumstances?
- Do you feel seen and heard by your partner? How would you change how you are seen and heard?
- Where is it most comfortable for you to express yourself with your partner? When is it most comfortable?
- What makes you uncomfortable about intimacy and being seen?

Questions to get you feeling and seeing (pick one or two):
- When you experience intimacy, what sensations do you feel in your body?
- If you feel shame in intimacy, where do you feel it physically? What does it feel like?

- In the past when you have felt validated, how did you feel then? How does it feel to remember and reflect upon that now?
- When you see other couples sharing intimate moments of deep connection, what dialogue is going on in your mind? How does it feel?
- What does it look like to be seen and heard by your partner? How does it feel?

To begin with, let's define "intimacy." What does it mean to you? Let's start with the elephant in the room: sex.

You can see where I'm going with this, right? Intimacy is most often thought of as sexual intimacy, and that's a piece of it, but it's not the whole picture. Not nearly. (I address sex and sensuality directly in a later chapter.)

Within wellness circles, intimacy is often expressed as: *In to me see.*

It's a sharing of yourself with someone else, allowing them to see into you as you look into them. It's deep. Profound. And it can trigger us like nothing else. James Cameron captured this essence of intimacy with his film *Avatar*. In the movie the indigenous Na'vi express intimacy with one another by saying "I see you." A very simple example executed beautifully in film.

We are at our most vulnerable when we are naked with another human being expressing ourselves openly and honestly. This does not mean you have to be having intercourse. Sexual intimacy transcends the act of sex itself. It can require more vulnerability to lie naked with another than to engage in sex. Lying naked includes those moments when we are baring our souls.

Of course, it can also include sexual interaction of any sort. I once had a male friend who shared with me that the moments he most cherished with his loved one were when she orgasmed, either with him or on her own. He said experiencing her orgasm was deeply intimate, because she was at her most real, raw, and authentic. In that moment, he knew who she was and saw into her. Into her heart. Profound.

For that reason, sex is often correlated with intimacy. Sexual intimacy is a powerful area to explore and can manifest in different ways. Some **What if..?** phrases to explore sexual intimacy may be:

What if I had better sex with my partner?

What if I had sex with my partner more often?

What if I were able to enjoy sex more with my partner?

What if I allowed myself to be seen more by my partner?

What if I initiated sexual activities more often?

What if I shared more of my desires and wishes with my partner?

Intimacy is not limited to sexual intimacy though, so let's take a look at some other forms of intimacy between two people.

When manifesting intimacy, we need to look at all the facets of a relationship and what it means to go deeper, to share, and to allow ourselves to be seen. Three big areas that come to mind are communication, trust, and respect.

Communication is a foundational element of any relationship. It goes without saying that you probably can't really have a healthy and intimate relationship with someone if you're not communicating. So, we won't address a situation where there is a lack of communication.

Where you can have a greater impact is on *how* you're choosing to communicate with one another. Therefore, the manifestation phrases to use around improving communication might look like this:

What if my partner and I set aside time to communicate regularly, without distraction, in an open and loving manner?

Or

What if my partner and I created more opportunities for loving communication that involved more listening and sharing?

Communication is at its best when it is consistent, mutually respectful, and adheres to agreed upon guidelines between the parties. That last bit is really the most important. The format for communication needs to be agreed upon, not imposed.

Think of it like this, if one person thinks they are communicating, because they are leaving Post-it notes everywhere for the other person, and the other person is not a Post-it note reader—there's no communication. The method for communicating needs to be accessible and functional for both individuals, otherwise it won't work. From there, creating opportunities through manifesting for greater communication becomes easier and helps to build a foundation of trust.

Trust is an interesting concept, and one I've wrestled with myself. Historically, I offered a whole lot of trust before it was necessarily earned. My professor from grad school, Brené Brown, had a great lesson on this with the Marble Jar.

Basically, we each have a marble jar in our relationships with other people; each time they do something to reinforce our trust in them, it's like they're putting a marble in our jar and/or we're putting one in theirs.

We wouldn't just hand over all of our marbles to someone without them earning them, would we? *(That would really be a case of losing your marbles!)*

This is what trust is all about—small, consistent actions built up over time to earn one another's ongoing and developing trust. And it's okay to start out offering a few marbles to someone if that feels right for you. A few marbles is not the entire jar.

With intimacy, what we're saying is that we are willing to continue to look further into each other, one marble at a time, building a foundation of trust.

Intimacy also requires **respect**. To continue with the marble jar:

Respecting each other's boundaries is key to the marble jar's existence. Let's say you like to give one marble for each event that reinforces the trust between you and your partner, but your partner is comfortable giving one marble for every three events. Both are equally valid. Respecting each other's pacing is what's key. One is not "right" and one "wrong." Both are boundaries, and both are true. Respect is what bridges the gap between two truths.

With communication, trust, and respect as the guideposts, we have new opportunities to create deeper intimacy with our partners. A lot of this comes from knowing yourself. In fact, I'd argue most of it does. Hence we completed the earlier exercises on beliefs and values. Each time you make a point of knowing yourself better, you create more opportunities for allowing others to know you and you to know them with deeper connection.

Now, let's apply the **What if..?** tool, which might look like this:

What if I learned what my own boundaries were and actively engaged in upholding them in my interactions with my partner?

What if I asked my partner about their boundaries and asked them to do the same?

What if I scheduled connection time with my partner, in which we created opportunities for communicating with one another as well as fun time?

What if I listened more often, and spoke less?

What if I asked my partner to share their dreams with me?

What if I shared my dreams with my partner?

I could go on and on. There are so many possibilities when it comes to intimacy and relationships with our partners. We could even extend this beyond partners to family and friends.

As you can see, intimacy can be a challenging subject. It's not easy to allow someone to see into your soul. It can be scary and exciting at the same time. In my experience it's almost always worth it, provided we keep in mind our own boundaries and well-being from the outset, as well as those of the other person.

In the end, though it may seem counter-intuitive, intimacy begins with the Self. It's harder to share yourself well with others if you don't know what you're sharing.

I invite you to know yourself, and find joy in sharing that knowing with others along the way.

CHAPTER 12

On Money and Wealth

"I'd like to live as a poor man with lots of money."

— Pablo Picasso —

What if..

You won the lottery?

Reminder: Let's start by answering a few questions to get you more connected with yourself. The goal is not to answer every question. Pick a couple that jump out at you and focus on those, knowing you can return to this chapter at a later date and look at other questions if you want to do more in-depth work.

Questions to get you thinking (pick one or two):

- What would you do with a windfall of cash?
- How would your life change? For the better? For worse?
- What opportunities could you create with more money?
- How would being wealthy change your life? Why?
- What preconceptions do you have about money and wealth? For yourself? For others?
- When you think about being wealthy, do you have a specific amount in mind? If so, what is it, and why?
- What does 'wealth' mean to you?
- How does stress and worry over finances play a role in your thoughts about wealth and money?

Questions to get you feeling and seeing (pick one or two):

- Imagine someone just gave you an extra $1000/month—how do you feel? What just happened in your body as you read that?

- Where in your body do you carry financial stress and worry?
- How does relief feel?
- If you were to build a comfortable retirement savings, what does that look like?
- How would it feel to know you are taken care of in retirement?

"Winning the lottery" might be the biggest and most often used **What if..?** phrase out there. We're always daydreaming about winning the lottery, aren't we? And if we barter enough with the Universe, we think it improves our odds.

We say things like: "If you let me win the lottery, I'll promise to give half of it away to charity. And then I'll build things for people, and then maybe I'll help someone else. Truly. I'll only keep some of it—think of all the good I'll do... if you let me win the lottery."

Sound familiar? If so, you're not alone. I've done it —and most everybody I know has done it. So, chances are, you've done it too. And that's okay. It's actually nice to know that in our manifesting we think of others and the good we can do if we get what we want. Kind of restores my faith in humanity a bit. I don't think it does a thing to improve our chances of actually winning the lottery, but it's nice to think about. We're back to daydreaming and using our imagination when we think about winning the lottery, and that's good. It's expansive. And anytime it includes benefitting others, well, I'm all in support of that.

Here's the thing though: What if you did win? Do you think it would magically change whatever struggle you're having internally? Do you think suddenly having a cash flow would impact your life so much that strife would be all but absent? Because if you do, you might not like what I have to say next.

You can't fix an internal problem with an external solution.

In other words: Money doesn't fix something that's broken inside.

Money, or wealth, provides. It provides opportunity and experience. Money helps us to create other things, things that we find to be fulfilling and validating. Money helps us get those things a little more easily and readily. Money buys us time, services, or creates space for healing, but it's not an actual "fix" for internal issues.

Don't get me wrong; money is great. Money helps us with our needs like paying bills, having a roof over our head, and eating. But winning the lottery isn't about that kind of money. That's different. Let's be sure to make that distinction.

When people are asking to win the lottery, it's not usually because they're not eating, though it can be for some. Most lottery players are playing because they deeply desire something to change in their life, and they believe an influx of cash would help precipitate that. The issue then is: What needs to change? What is out of alignment that having lots of money would "fix?"

Another way to ask that is: *What is broken inside that needs to be healed?*

I have no problem with manifesting wealth and abundance. I think it's great. What matters is the energy and intention behind the manifesting. If the desire for wealth is to compensate for an area of scarcity, fear or lack, then the wealth is most likely not going to happen. Not until the underlying fear with the emotional deficit is addressed.

Therefore, let's look at two common reasons for manifesting wealth or abundance:

1. Manifesting abundance for security and stability.

2. Manifesting wealth for creativity.

To begin, when we're manifesting abundance, we need to address the pre-existing thought patterns around scarcity as I've just mentioned. I could tell you there's always enough for everybody, but telling you isn't the same as you knowing it. My telling you doesn't unravel the thought patterns that keep you bound. So, let's address scarcity.

Scarcity is a belief. Understanding that is key to addressing it. Yes, there is poverty, famine, and disease. There are a lot of things that reinforce the notion that scarcity is a truth, but it's not. It's a belief, and a belief is not the same as a truth. If you believe that there is not enough, there won't be. Ever. If you believe there is enough, it becomes a possibility. Do you see the difference?

One belief eliminates possibility while the other creates it, and that's what we're talking about. Possibility.

When we're manifesting abundance and wealth, we're putting our eggs in the basket of possibility and saying, "Yes, please!" We're not eradicating homelessness or hunger (though that would be nice). Let's start with changing our own lives for the stronger, and then allow that to radiate out into our communities and society as a whole. As the old oxygen mask theory goes: You can't help someone else to breathe if you're not breathing yourself.

Manifesting abundance for stability or security is about saying to the Universe: "I desire freedom." Think about it. If you're desperate for more money in order to pay your bills, then you're asking for something from a mindset of fear and scarcity. If, however, you're asking for more in order to liberate yourself from limitation and feel more secure, then you're talking about freedom. The Universe likes freedom. It's all about free will and freedom. It will respond, and you don't get to control the "how."

So, to manifest abundance for freedom, you're going to ask a very different **What if..?** question than you'd ask if you were manifesting the money to pay bills out of fear or lack. Manifesting for freedom looks like this:

What if I had more than enough financial resources to meet my needs, and then some?

Instead of:

What if I had enough money this month to pay my bills?

By using the first phrase, you are giving the Universe two options on how to address your request. It can either a) decrease your needs, or b) increase your resources. Its options just doubled. Again, the "how" isn't your business; it's the Universe's. Let it do its job.

Manifesting wealth for creativity is even more powerful because it's basically telling the Universe you want to play—and it's all for that! In fact, if you think of the Universe as a giant sand box, without actual borders, it's filled with kids creating, building, and laughing. It's joy-filled and contagious. So when you say "Hey, I want to play too," the Universe starts doing a jig and dancing in the sand as it makes room for you.

Saying you want to play is like raising your hand and jumping up when a volunteer is called for. It's vastly more empowering for both parties. What does it look like to say you want to play? Something like this:

What if I created a totally new way to fix/do/help with X?

What if I developed a product that helped others who needed it?

What if I shared what I've learned and it helped people?

What if I provided opportunities for creativity in others?

What if I were rewarded for all these fun, creative, life-changing things?

These are unspecific examples. They can cross any industry or profession. They are infinite in their capacity to change the world and your abundance and wealth.

But then, what would something specific look like? Let's use me as an example again:

What if I wrote a book that was compelling, well-received, and helped others to change their lives for the better while providing me with a steady income stream that allowed me to create more books, workshops, and teachings, expanding the ripples of change even further? And, **What if** that book, and all my subsequent books, became a bestseller?

Yes, I added that last "bestseller" bit. Why? Well, why not? **What if** this book or any subsequent book I write became a bestseller? Would it change my life? Would it change other people's lives? For the better? Even if it's just one person or one thought pattern, the answer is yes and yes. And yes! And that's always a good thing.

Change is the Universe in action. It's the essence of possibility and manifestation. Change is good.

In order to create abundance and wealth, as in so many other areas of manifesting, we need to focus on the reason behind the desire for change. I've said it before, and I'll say it again: Intention matters. Your reason for wanting something is always valid. Understanding the energy behind it and coming to your **What if..?** phrase positively and authentically is what's most important.

You want to be a millionaire? Great! Manifest it. Just manifest it knowing why you want to be a millionaire. Money isn't a solution to inner conflict. It can help you get help, support, and information, but it isn't a long-term solution and it never will be if there is an underlying problem out of alignment. In that regard, money is a tool. If you see it as a tool to accomplish something that is in alignment with your values and authenticity, you will have greater success in manifesting your dreams, including wealth and abundance.

CHAPTER 13

On Health

"If we are creating ourselves all the time,
then it is never too late to begin creating
the bodies we want instead of the ones
we mistakenly assume we are stuck with."

— Deepak Chopra —

What if..

You were healthier?

Reminder: Let's start by answering a few questions to get you more connected with yourself. The goal is

not to answer every question. Pick a couple that jump out at you and focus on those, knowing you can return to this chapter at a later date and look at other questions if you want to do more in-depth work.

Questions to get you thinking (pick one or two):
- What does it mean to be healthy?
- Think of the healthiest person you know, what about them do you admire?
- If you could only change one aspect of your health, what would it be? Why?
- If your overall health were quantifiable, on a scale of 0–100, how healthy do you think you are? Why?
- How willing are you to invest in yourself?
- What is the strongest aspect of your health routine?

Questions to get you feeling and seeing (pick one or two):
- Where and how do you feel well in your body? And unwell?
- When you engage in physical activity, how do you feel? How do you want to feel?

- Daily practices encourage good health, so imagine having the necessary time to commit to a daily routine; what would that look like?

- When you are feeling your healthiest and strongest, what do you wear?

- What does eating well taste like? Feel like?

Unfortunately, this is one of those areas where we have a tendency to use the destructive energy of the **What if..?** phrase more than the creative power it wields. When we're sick or struggling, it often shows up like this:

What if I get sick?

What if I get cancer?

What if I lose my battle?

What if I can't do X, Y, or Z?

What if my treatment doesn't work?

What if I die?

I think I've said enough of that, and I'll add the "cancel and purify" phrase again here. Those are all realistic fears, grounded in true emotion, especially when we get sick and feel weak. I'm not saying don't have the fear. It's real if you feel it. Feeling our emotions is part of being healthy. Shoving them out of the way and ignoring them is not.

What I am saying is that when that fear arises, don't feed it. Feeding it looks like those questions above. Now, let me be clear, I've done this too. There's no "perfect" here. There's only change, over time, with intention.

The fear needs to be addressed, preferably with a good support system, like a support group or a therapist, while the possibility for something else is being created from within. This is where hope plays a vital role in drafting your **What if..?** phrase.

Instead of asking the fear-based question, *focus on the possibility-based question*. Such as:

What if I healed completely?

That's a really good phrase actually, as it's active, all-encompassing, and definitive.

In no way are we disregarding the fear. We are choosing to manifest something greater than fear.

I know many people that have experienced serious illness. In my own family, we've dealt with some major life changes due to illness, and it's never easy. Manifesting something different is a challenge—one that can be daunting to the most practiced individual, and there's a difference between manifesting health for yourself and for someone else. We're back to the issue of free will.

When we, ourselves, are sick, manifesting something different can be powerful medicine. Living in the space of hope and possibility can, quite literally, change our physical bodies. It's truly amazing what we can achieve. There are countless stories around of people who have used the power of intention and possibility to change their physical life circumstances. (Louise Hay has an extraordinary story and has been a pioneer in the realm of mind-body wellness.) Similarly, there are also many stories of people who have succumbed to one illness or another, sometimes even when they were manifesting a different outcome.

- Will manifesting create opportunities for miracles? I believe it does.
- Will manifesting save someone from a terminal diagnosis? Perhaps, and perhaps not—I've seen both.
- Will it change the course of Alzheimer's in a patient? I don't know.

There's not enough research that's been done yet on all these areas of mind-body wellness. Thankfully, though, there is some, and it shows promise and offers hope. *(One such resource is Dr. Andrew Newberg, who is a pioneer in the study of neurotheology. For more, check out his website at www.andrewnewberg.com.)*

Now, let's address the issue of manifesting wellness for someone else. As with everything, you can't manifest for others. You can hope for others, and pray for others, and add your collective energy to their healing process —and I believe that all works and plays a role in whether someone gets better or not. But, at the end of the day, you can't alter someone else's free will. If the patient does not want to get better, or isn't willing to engage in their own healing, that's their choice.

I know this is a touchy subject. From personal experience, I understand how frustrating it can be to sit by and watch someone you love get sicker, especially when they are unwilling to help themselves. It's awful and can leave you feeling both helpless and hopeless. Those two feelings create a prime opportunity for wanting to jump in and change things for someone else. My cautionary tale is simply this:

Manifesting wellness for others has the potential to impede your own health.

We see it all the time when caregivers end up sicker than their wards. When this happens, it's important to redirect your energies and make sure you're not giving your life force over to someone who doesn't actually want to get better. It's the old oxygen mask theory of care again. You can't help someone put on their oxygen mask if you don't have yours on first.

It's also a red flag in my world of coaching, therapy, and energy work. When I see someone pouring all their energy into impacting someone else's free will, my warning signals go off.

And sometimes, no matter how much someone wants to get better and uses every tool offered to them, they don't get better. It feels unfair, and it hurts. It's not something that's easily explained or under-stood. Not everything is explainable or understandable. Sometimes this happens, and when it does it's okay to hurt. It's always okay to feel your feelings. It only becomes problematic (unhealthy) when you attach to them and begin to identify with them.

∞

As for manifesting your own health, that's very different. We've already touched on this topic in an earlier chapter, but let's delve deeper into what it means to be healthy.

To begin with, there are four aspects of health. Historically, we've heard about the three-pronged mind-body-spirit approach to wellness. Recently, though, I've seen more and more people talking and writing about the four-pronged approach that I prefer to use, and have for several years. These are:

- Mental health
- Emotional health
- Physical health
- Spiritual health

Previously, mental and emotional health had been lumped together into "mind"—but they're very different and need to be addressed individually.

Mental health is about cognitive functioning in your daily life. How are your thoughts affecting your behavior? Are they? *(Hint: They are. Always.)* Are you consciously walking through life, or are you walking around semi-awake?

This is the "respond or react" paradigm. A response is a thoughtful and considered reply to some stimulus. It's authentic and honest, and it comes from a predominantly emotion-neutral place. Reacting, on the other hand, is usually emotionally charged. It's the reply given in haste or anger. It's the knee-jerk response that often leads to emotional regret or emotional hangover, and it rarely includes cognitive processing.

So, mental health starts with learning and understanding your cognitive wellness, and then doing your best to raise your awareness to the unhealthy thought patterns and their subsequent behaviors. Mental health is about choice.

What that means is that we create our thought patterns—both negative and positive. Each time we choose follow the same pattern, we reinforce it. It's like creating a trail in the woods. The more often it gets walked on, the harder the surface becomes and the less vegetation grows. It becomes "cemented."

Thought patterns are the same. The more often we have them and use them, the more cemented they become, whether "good" or "bad." (Hence the guideline for consistency and repetition at the beginning of the book.) Let's deliberately cement the good ones.

Mental health then becomes a matter of awareness, consistency, and deliberate action. What thoughts are you having? How are they affecting you? What do you want to change?

Emotional health is a little different, though it also originates in your head. Emotional health lies more in the reptilian brain. It's the fight-flight-freeze neural center of the brain. Not only does it reside in the brain, but it extends to your entire body.

Think about the last time you felt really happy. Where did you feel it? In your head? Or did you also feel it in your belly? Your chest? Your face? Did your toes curl with excitement from something? There's a reason we have metaphors like "butterflies in the stomach" to explain and express an emotion—because we feel it, physically. And that's a good thing. It's our body's way of saying, "Hey! Take note!"

Many thousands of years ago, that emotional center kept us alive. Not only did it protect us from marauding lions *(Yep, I said that!)*, but it also encouraged us to procreate and continue our species. (There's a reason your heart "skips a beat" and your nether-regions tingle at the sight of your lover.) All of these things combine to create one heck of a system. So, what happens when it's not functioning optimally? Well, sickness occurs. Or as many wellness professionals have termed it: dis-ease.

Dis-ease means we are out of ease with our emotions and their excellent notification system. Emotional health, therefore, is about re-aligning ourselves with our whole Self. It's about learning how and why the emotional system functions as it does, and allowing ourselves to cooperate with it and participate fully in its wisdom.

Speaking of participation, **physical health** is all about participation.

I'm going to be honest here: This has been my weakest link in my wellness strategy. As I write this book, I am working to change that and turn it around step by step. (Literally: I'm walking more.) It's going well, and I'm glad to report that I can see the forest and the trees. Here's what I've learned about physical health: It matters. A lot.

Even if we don't have the obvious symptoms of a diagnosis, when we're not functioning at our best physically, it affects the other areas of wellness, and vice versa.

What I've come to learn in exploring my own physical health is that I can't meditate through gastrointestinal distress if I don't address the physical cause as well. Just as you can't fix an internal problem with an external solution, the opposite is also true: you can't fix an external (physical) problem with a solely internal solution.

Using the tools from the other (non-physical) areas of wellness to address physical wellness can help or alleviate symptoms, but it doesn't necessarily change our physical state. The goal here is change, not alleviation.

Physical health requires the additional use of tools that directly address the physical body. For me that meant small changes in my eating as well as walking more. I'm being deliberate about my choices in small steps. Small steps, over time, lead to BIG changes. Plus, they're more likely to last. For you it might mean something else. To understand this better, it's important to be open to working with an expert in this field. This is what I have done, and I highly recommend it.

Together, my holistic doctor Tom and I are incorporating all four aspects of wellness, through the lens of the physical, his specialty. He's very supportive and knowledgeable in the areas in which I don't feel up to speed yet, and understands that health incorporates all four aspects. We examine my physical health as well as the other three components, and work together to create new behaviors and routines that support all four areas. It's a great approach, and it provides me with an extensive toolbox to create the life I imagine. Every day.

"Every day" is a phrase that also underscores **spiritual health**. For many, this can be a challenging subject. Let's break it down.

Spiritual does not mean religion. It does mean to reconnect, which is actually a possible Latin root of the word "religion" (re-ligare). So, when we discuss spirituality and exclude religion, we may be throwing the baby out with the bath water.

Historically, religions have been a way for people to reconnect to that which they know, feel, or believe. When groups of people gathered to reconnect, practices were formed. These practices turned into the religions we see today. Often, it's the practices and surrounding hierarchy that people react to when we discuss the word "religion"—not necessarily the feeling or intention behind the belief or reconnection.

For me, "religion" isn't bad, and it's interchangeable with "spirituality" because of the inherent meaning in each word. For the purposes of this book, I use spirituality because it's simply more accepted and understood.

Spiritual health, therefore, is about connection. To begin with, it's about connecting to a greater power. Some call it God, others call it Nature, Higher Power, Source, or the Universe. There are infinite ways to describe the connection we seek to that which is outside of ourselves—and also contained within us. To make it easy, I'll use the terms God or the Universe. Replace it with whatever works for you.

Connecting to God, and the God essence that is within you, creates three things: love, faith, and hope. The energy of these emotions is highly creative and infinite. When you look at a flower pushing through the soil after a particularly long or hard winter, what do you feel? Hope? Love? Joy? Faith?

This is spirituality. This is spiritual health.

Taking time to reconnect with everything around you is integral to spiritual health.

There's another connection to be made that encompasses the previous three areas of wellness we've discussed as well: Connection to Self.

Spiritual health includes a connection to the Self, with a capital "S." It's this connection that enables us to access our awareness and intuition, which we use in each of the aforementioned areas of health. Without this access, any sort of path to health becomes more challenging.

Some refer to this as a "sixth sense" or a "knowing." You know when you're getting sick, often before the fever hits. You just feel "off." You know when someone you love has been in an accident. Or you know when your child gets hurt before you get the phone call.

Speaking of phone calls, how many of you know who is calling before you answer the phone or see who it is? This is spiritual connection. It's a presence of Self in the midst of human experience. We nurture it through practices, alone or in community. We incorporate it in our daily routine, often without realizing it (Think of the last time you smiled at nature—that's spirituality.)

Spiritual health, therefore, is presence and connection. It's awareness and openness to possibility.

∞

Now that we've addressed the four major areas of wellness, the question is: How do we manifest greater health in our lives?

Through balance.

Wellness is achieved through a balancing of the four components of health. So, we're going to go back to the beginning of the book and look at the exercises we completed around thought patterns and values.

With our lists in hand, we will look at our values through the lenses of mental, emotional, physical, and spiritual health. Where we are out of alignment, we create a **What if..?** phrase to manifest greater balance. It looks something like this:

For me, I was out of alignment with my physical health, as I've mentioned. For years, I put a lot of effort into strengthening the other three areas, somewhat to the detriment of my physical wellness. In order to regain balance, in addition to working with a professional, I created a manifestation phrase around physical health. This was the first phrase I used:

What if I felt better?

From there, I expanded it to:

What if I felt strong?

What if I woke up each day feeling strong and healthy?

What if I developed a daily routine that incorporated all aspects of health?

What if I created more opportunities for myself to choose healthy options that supported my feeling strong and healthy in balance with the four aspects of wellness?

As I progressed through each variation of my **What if..?** phrase, I created more opportunities for physical health and wellness in my life. And it continues to evolve to this day, as I do. Perhaps the most important thing about manifesting is being open to changing your manifesting as you change.

What will your phrase be? Where are you out of balance, and where would you like to create positive change? All it takes is one little step to get going, and you're on your way. Hooray!

CHAPTER 14

On Sexuality and Sensuality

*"Touch me, touch the palm of your
hand to my body as I pass,
Be not afraid of my body."*

— Walt Whitman —

What if..

You expressed yourself sexually without fear or shame?

Reminder: Let's start by answering a few questions to get you more connected with yourself. The goal is

not to answer every question. Pick a couple that jump out at you and focus on those, knowing you can return to this chapter at a later date and look at other questions if you want to do more in-depth work.

Questions to get you thinking (pick one or two):
- How do you express yourself sexually?
- What is your favorite sexual activity?
- When you fantasize about sexual freedom, what do you think about?
- How does your sexuality and sensuality show up in your life?
- Do you have pre-existing beliefs around sexuality and sensuality? About yourself? About others?
- How do you express your sexual desires with your partner? Yourself?

Questions to get you feeling and seeing (pick one or two):
- When you are feeling sexy and confident, how do you walk?
- How is it different from how you walk when you're feeling sensually repressed?
- What does an orgasm feel like to you?

- If you close your eyes and imagine your most sexually liberating moment, what was it? Where did you feel it in your body? In your mind? What did it look like?
- When you see yourself naked in the mirror, do you feel sensual? Why? Why not?
- If you could wear one thing that makes you feel confident in your sensuality, what would it be? Why?

In earlier chapters we discussed intimacy, sexual intimacy, and relationships with others and ourselves. By now there should be a clear definition of intimacy that can involve sex, but isn't necessarily about sex. Sexuality and sensuality, on the other hand, are all about sexual expression. This may or may not involve a partner, which is what makes it inherently different than intimacy. This is about your personal relationship to sex and how healthy it is.

Some of you may think to stop reading now as this isn't in your sphere or reality at this point in your life. Indeed, that was some of the feedback I received during my beta testing. This section didn't apply to some of my readers. Perhaps you're the same. You're single or this chapter of your life is in your past. I'm going to suggest you keep reading, though.

Why? Because this chapter explores a very important aspect of the human experience. Our relationship with sex is externally influenced on a daily basis whether you realize it or not. So, it's my opinion that it's very important to know and understand your relationship with sex if for no other reason than to be able to weed through the daily influx of sexually-related material and formulate your own healthy opinion and attitude.

To be clear, I'm not talking about sexual identity or gender identity. I'm not an expert on those topics and wouldn't begin to attempt to explore them in a meaningful way. I know how important they are to discuss and understand in a respectful manner.

I am talking about sex, sensuality, and the personal relationship we have with both. That means, in some ways I'm also talking about sexual repression. Sexual repression has played a role in undermining sexual self-expression for ages.

Going back to sensuality and sex, what does it mean to manifest greater sensuality and sexual expression? What does that look like?

In my opinion, it's liberating. Being able to safely and openly express and share yourself can be a life-affirming experience. I'm talking about the possibility of fully embodying your Self, including your sexual self, without fear.

I once heard a woman tell another woman that she "oozed sex." For some reason, this wasn't well received. Perhaps the woman saying it was in some way demeaning and belittling the other woman's existence to something primal. Or perhaps it was because the other woman was very uncomfortable with the thought that she "oozed" anything.

From my perspective, I could see what the statement was trying—albeit failing—to say. The second woman did indeed "ooze sex." That is to say, she was very comfortable in her skin, which included her sexuality and sensuality. She couldn't help but express it in everything she did. It was in her walk, in her talk, and in the way she wore her clothes. Now, before you go off thinking she walked around in skimpy tight things and had a body fat percentage of less than 10, let me reframe it for you.

The second woman was of larger-than-average build. She wore jeans or khakis and t-shirts or sweaters. Her favorite shoes were flats or boots. This was the 90's, and jeans were mostly tapered, sometimes whitewashed, and often came from menswear. In fact, she wore men's Levi's. And yet, she oozed sex. Why? Because she had come to know her own body.

This was, actually, one of the first things she ever shared with me about her sexual knowing. "You have to know your own body," she said. "Otherwise, why are you sharing it with someone if you're not willing to know it yourself?"

There was no shame in her self-expression, no feeling of being "lesser-than" or "not enough." She didn't hide her physique under baggy clothes, and she didn't exploit it either. Nothing about her was about sexual repression or expression. Everything about her was about *her* and the confidence she held as she moved through life.

That's the key here. Sexual expression and sensuality are about *you*, not somebody else's perception of you and what they want you to look like or be. Nor are they about some external measurement of what's "sexy." Magazines are made to sell advertising and ideas; they're not meant to make you feel satisfied and happy exactly as you are, because then why would you want to spend money to change yourself in order to feel better?

What I'm asking here is for you to begin a healthy relationship with yourself on what your idea of sensuality is, and what makes you feel most confident in your whole being.

When it comes to manifesting greater confidence or comfort in your sensuality, it has to focus on you and only you. It cannot focus on what an external voice (your spouse/partner/lover or society) says or wants. In order to get there, we need to identify the gaps around how you feel about yourself sexually.

To bring it back to the tangible, here's what that could look like using **What if..?**:

What if I listened to my body?

What if I explored my body?

What if I expressed myself physically and sexually?

What if I asked for what I needed?

What if I explored my sexual interests?

What if I paid attention to my own needs?

What if I felt comfortable in my body?

I'd like to add: **What if** *you* accepted you, exactly as you are? And how would it feel if someone else accepted you, exactly as you are? What freedom would you experience? How would you be better able to express yourself?

Now let's go a little deeper: Sexual expression.

For many people, the thought of being sexually adventurous is both exciting and scary. I also know people who think anything outside of what they are comfortable with is perverse. Both are equally valid.

Both are true because it's their truth, even if one doesn't understand the other. What's important is that we don't impose our values on someone else.

Quite recently an erotic novel has become a surprising bestseller. Why is that? With our media full of sex for decades, if not centuries, why is it shocking to have an erotic bestseller?

In my opinion, one of the reasons *50 Shades of Grey* has caused an uproar is because the main character, Christian Grey, is quite comfortable—if not wholly confident—in his sexuality. He knows who he is, what he likes and wants. I think that's one of the reasons why the book has been so successful. It spoke to something inside of us that perhaps we crave: freedom of sexual expression, however that shows up for each of us.

Sexual expression is unique to each individual. No one person has the right or ability to tell another what is acceptable and pleasurable. Therefore, to label someone else as "perverse" or "wrong" in some way is to deny his or her humanity. We have thousands of years of documented sexual history to give us evidence that sexual expression is part of humanity. Even a lack of sexual expression, or the choice to be asexual, is an expression of Self and sexuality. Therefore, to deny our sexuality is to chop off a part of what it means to be human.

To be blunt, sexual expression is one of the great joys of being human, especially if you think about it from this perspective: When we are in spirit form we are denied both the pleasures and pain of the flesh. That means that we can't enjoy the taste and feel of chocolate as it melts on our tongue, nor can we experience the rush and ecstasy of orgasm. It also means that we don't feel the pain of loss when someone dies or the suffering that accompanies injury or illness.

For me, being human is entirely about experiencing the good and the bad, and I consider it all a gift. One of those gifts is sexual expression and the freedom that accompanies it (and of course the chocolate!)

Fitting in to someone else's expectation of you, sexually, is to limit and cage yourself. Is it easy to break out of that cage? Not always, but it's possible. It begins with a conversation with yourself.

What do you like? Enjoy?

What don't you enjoy?

Would you dance naked for yourself? For your lover?

Would you watch them dance naked for you, with love and joy in your heart?

What are your fantasies? What are your lover's fantasies?

These are just a few questions to get you thinking about your own relationship to sexuality and sensuality —a necessary exercise before manifesting something different.

Once you have a solid understanding (or at least a better understanding) of your own sexual expression and desires, manifesting change is the next step. How this translates and what this might look like could be:

What if I opened myself up to freer sexual expression in how I interact with my lover?

What if I allowed myself to learn, explore, and experience deeper sexual satisfaction?

What if I shared my sexual fantasies with my lover and asked them to do the same?

What if I looked at myself naked in the mirror and felt loving and sexual?

What if I accepted my body and my desires exactly as they are right now, and asked for my needs to be met?

Sexuality and sensuality are not easy topics. Even though it's rampant in our society, it's still taboo in our discussions. Why? It can be one of the greatest pleasures in our lives, and yet we're scared to speak up for our needs and ourselves.

Change starts with a conversation, an honest conversation, with yourself. From there, anything is possible.

CHAPTER 15

On Material Possessions

*"It is the preoccupation with possessions,
more than anything else, that prevents
us from living freely and nobly."*

— *Bertrand Russell* —

What if..

You had that 'one thing' you always wanted?

Reminder: Let's start by answering a few questions
to get you more connected with yourself. The goal is
not to answer every question. Pick a couple that jump

out at you and focus on those, knowing you can return to this chapter at a later date and look at other questions if you want to do more in-depth work.

Questions to get you thinking (pick one or two):

- What do you think is missing from your life?
- What is your favorite possession? Why? What does it mean to you?
- What value do you place on your material possessions? Is the value yours? Or externalized?
- When was the last time you bought something for yourself solely out of need, not want? When was it want? Was there a difference in how it felt?
- What does it mean to "own" something? A house? A car?
- What are you telling yourself about the importance of ownership?

Questions to get you feeling and seeing (pick one or two):

- If you lost everything to a natural disaster, how would you feel? Where do you feel it in your body? How do you picture yourself?

- When you see or think about that most cherished possession, what does your body do? How do you feel?
- Picture having that "one thing" you've always wanted. How do you feel? Are you smiling? What is going on in your gut?
- If someone gave you a gift that you've always wanted, how would they say you responded? What would they say you looked like?

A few years ago, the fire alarm in my apartment building went off. I thought it was an error until I saw the fire doors slam shut in the hallway and smoke billowing out of a neighbor's apartment. In the millisecond it took me to process what I was seeing, I made a decision.

I grabbed my car keys, my mobile phone, and my dog, and I left. While I was standing outside watching the fire department pull up with their sirens blaring, I started chatting with the woman next to me. She lived two floors below me, and we had never met. In her hurry to leave, she forgot her purse, her keys, and her phone. She turned to me and said, "You're so smart. You grabbed your phone."

At the time, I was thinking to myself how I really only cared about grabbing my dog, but I acknowledged her kind comment and smiled. What happened next was really one of the most important lessons in my life.

As I watched the firemen scamper about the stairwells, and as other neighbors gathered to discuss what was going on, I listened to my neighbor lament her decisions and fear for her belongings. In that moment, I realized that I didn't actually have significant attachments to my belongings anymore. Yes, I would miss them if they were gone, and I'd be more sad about some of them than others, but what mattered more to me than anything was the fact that I got out with my dog, an ability to leave the area (car keys), and a way to stay connected with friends and family (phone). The rest didn't really matter. I felt complete.

It's been years since that event, and thankfully, the damage was minor. In moments since then, I can honestly say that I've lamented the loss of some items in my life. Why? Because they made me smile. And that, right there, is the only reason to manifest possessions, in my opinion.

If something will contribute to your life in a meaningful way, then go for it. If, however, it will add burden and stress because you associate it with some external measurement of approval or acceptance, then perhaps it's best not to manifest a new house or a new car.

Using a barometer of happiness, joy, or meaning is key to this section of manifesting. If you want a bigger yard because of what you think people will think of you, then it may not be a great idea to manifest it —because a bigger yard will never fill your need for approval. If, however, you want a bigger yard because you can grow more vegetables, or you can play with your kids, or any other thing that brings you joy, then it's probably more in alignment with your values. *(See? There are those values again.)*

Manifesting material possessions has been a focus of many authors and teachers in recent times. There are a good number of books out there that teach you how to get the things you want using the Law of Attraction. It's good because it's an easy way to see the fruits of your practice. It's tangible. But if the goal we're aiming for is a better life, lived in greater alignment with our values, filled with joy, peace, and wellness, then manifesting possessions needs to be entered into somewhat delicately.

Therefore, the biggest question to ask yourself when manifesting possessions is: Why? As in: Why do I want this thing? What do I think it will bring me?

As a result, the **What if..?** phrase to use regarding possessions might look like this:

What if I lived in a place that made me happy each day as I woke up and looked outside?

What if I lived in a supportive community?

What if I drove a car that was reliable? That I enjoyed?

What if every item of clothing I owned was easy and comfortable to wear and made me feel good each time I looked in the mirror?

As you can see, this becomes more about the feelings generated by the item than about the item itself.

In truth, I'd love to have a little piece of land somewhere with a small house and a garden, where I could walk my dog off-leash through the surrounding countryside and come home to a deep bathtub under a glass roof. I think that sounds like perfection. In fact, I'm manifesting it regularly because I believe in it and can see it in my mind very clearly.

Everything about what I just wrote has to do with the feeling that such a location will give me. The garden will nurture my body and soul while the surrounding countryside will support my creative process in my mind and help me stay physically fit and recharged. As for the hot bath under a starry sky—I don't know, it just makes me smile.

That's what manifesting possessions is all about —inviting what makes you smile into your life for a while.

So, smile as you make your list, enjoy your day-dreaming, and fill yourself with *gratitude* as your dreams become reality.

Final Thoughts

*"The quality of your life is based
on the choices you make."*

— *Martina E. Faulkner* —

The idea of manifesting has created interesting re-
actions. I've heard it referred to as witchcraft,
hocus-pocus, materialistic, selfish, and bogus, to
name a few. I've also heard it referred to as powerful,
captivating, empowering, liberating, and life-changing.

The difference lies in how it's understood and used.

Just like the **What if..?** phrase, manifesting holds a
duality in its essence, and just like the phrase, the

power lies with the user. Our minds are more powerful than we may realize for both the good and the bad. The bad seems to happen automatically with some of our ingrained beliefs and negative thought patterns. We have the power to change that. Then, amazingly, we have the power to create something different.

That is the beauty of manifestation: It is creative. And creativity is infinite.

As for me, I manifest everything from phone calls or emails to business opportunities and wellness. I've given you a few examples throughout this text to help you see the theory in practice. I've been using it personally for years, professionally with my clients, and as part of my guided meditations and workshops. At times I've sat back in awe at what I've been able to do. (And at other times I've pouted when the Universe knew better.) Additionally, there have been times when I have walked away from manifesting out of fear of its power. Or, perhaps that's better said: *my* power with *it*.

I've learned to adopt a healthy attitude about manifesting by understanding the Universal Law of free will and the basic premise of spiritual alignment. Since then, it has been both a tool and a toy. It's fun! I enjoy "testing" it out now and then, and I have also used it to get serious about changing the world, inviting my Facebook community to engage in manifesting practices where better outcomes are needed. Why not harness our connection and community for the betterment of all?

Its power is truly limitless, and the more we practice using our imagination, the more elastic and expansive it becomes. Anything—truly anything—becomes possible.

In this book, I have shared some of the wisdom learned through the years in relationship to manifesting. I say some because the topic is endless, and keeping this text simple, concise, and clear is what makes sense to me. Why? Because it is an invitation to create change. Remember, *small steps lead to great and lasting change.*

As I've said before, this isn't rocket science, though it could create all sorts of possibilities to open us up to even more explorations of the Universe. So, in a way, maybe it is...

Resources

When I mention resources in my writing I like to share that information with others. If I did not reference it in the text itself, I am offering it here. In alignment with my value of holding other people up, here is a short list of the people/resources I mentioned in this book (in order of appearance). Check them out if you're interested.

Introduction and Chapter 10:

José Luis Stevens, PhD—The Power Path School of Shamanism.

www.thepowerpath.com

Chapters 5 and 11:

Brené Brown, PhD, LMSW; The Marble Jar is explained in her book *Daring Greatly,* among others. Brené also uses a variation of the values exercise in her workshop The Daring Way™.
www.thedaringway.com
www.brenebrown.com

Chapter 13:

Dr. Tom Bayne—Pure Balance Natural Family Healthcare.
www.pbhealthcenter.com

Dr. Andrew Newberg—Jefferson University Hospital.
www.andrewnewberg.com

Finally, if you'd like to attend a **What If..? Workshop** with me, or organize one for your own group or organization, visit my website www.martinafaulkner.com to learn more and/or to contact me. I look forward to hearing from you!

About the Author

As an author and Life Coach, Martina's goal is to inspire and assist others in creating a meaningful and joy-filled life. Ever the student, Martina E. Faulkner, LMSW, is constantly exploring, learning, and creating multi-faceted approaches to wellness that work.

Martina's training as a certified Life Coach, psychotherapist, and Reiki Master Teacher sets her apart in the wellness industry, guiding her to conceive powerful, life-changing workshops and books.

Whether it's developing customized guided meditations, using her intuitive gifts to connect with the Universe, or reaching into her tool bag for coaching or psychotherapeutic interventions, Martina establishes a dynamic space in which her readers and clients are supported and called upon to grow and excel.

Martina has conducted workshops for corporations, non-profit organizations, women's groups, and individuals. Through these workshops and one-on-one sessions, she teaches her clients how to actualize a more meaningful, healthy, and joy-filled life. Most recently, Martina has developed the *What If..?* workshop in order to share and apply the teachings in this book.

Martina currently resides in the Chicagoland area with her family and her dog. She writes weekly for her blog, InspireBytes™, and enjoys being in nature or pursuing her creative outlets, such as photography, painting, and jewelry making.

www.martinafaulkner.com
www.inspirebytes.com